WORKBOOK *for*

Explorations

An Introduction to Astronomy

THIRD EDITION

Published *for the*

UNITED STATES AIR FORCE
JUNIOR RESERVE OFFICER TRAINING CORPS

V-7326W

The McGraw-Hill Companies, Inc.

Boston   Burr Ridge, IL   Dubuque, IA   Madison, WI   New York
San Francisco   St. Louis   Bangkok   Bogotá   Caracas   Kuala Lumpur
Lisbon   London   Madrid   Mexico City   Milan   Montreal   New Delhi
Santiago   Seoul   Singapore   Sydney   Taipei   Toronto

WORKBOOK for

Explorations: An Introduction to Astronomy

This book is a McGraw-Hill Custom Publishing textbook and contains select material from *Explorations: An Introduction to Astronomy*, Third Edition by Thomas T. Arny. Copyright © 2004, 2002, 2000 by The McGraw-Hill Companies, Inc. Reprinted with permission of the publisher. Many custom published texts are modified versions or adaptations of our best-selling textbooks. Some adaptations are printed in black and white to keep prices at a minimum, while others are in color.

Instructor materials were created by Coyote Enterprises, Inc. 14 Thayer Road Colorado Springs, Colorado 80906 using materials from *Explorations in Space: an Introduction to Astronomy* by Thomas T. Arny, and its *Instructor Materials, Online Learning Center,* and *Digital Content Manager.* The revised instructor materials, including the PowerPoint slides, student workbook and instructor guide were created by Joel Miller, Perry Luckett, Doug Kirkpatrick, Jerry Sellers and Wiley Larson under the guidance of LTC John Kiecana and Roger Ledbetter.

3 4 5 6 7 8 9 0 PAH PAH 0 9 8 7 6

ISBN 0-07-312778-7

Custom Publishing Editor: Judith Wetherington
Production Editor: Carrie Braun
Cover Design: Fairfax Hutter
Printer/Binder: The P.A. Hutchison Company

CONTENTS

Preface

Introduction

Explorations An Introduction to Astronomy is an exciting textbook about astronomy. Together with the text, the workbook will guide you through the history of astronomy, a closer look at Earth and the Moon, a tour of our solar system, and a peek at the cosmos.

By applying yourself to these learning aids, you can find great insights into why people have been fascinated with the heavens since the beginning of human life on Earth. What you learn here not only will ready you for other courses in astronomy and aerospace engineering but also will make you a better observer of the world and sky around you.

Student Strategy

Lessons 1 and 6 don't have a reading assignment, so you have only an in-class presentation from which to learn. You can answer the questions in this Workbook for those lessons by reading the slides and listening carefully to your instructor.

The text covers a lot of material. We recommend you read the assigned sections and pages in the text, answer the questions in this Workbook, and then listen to your teacher's presentation, take notes, and participate in class. By seeing most of the material three times, you'll learn more and remember it longer.

Workbook Layout

For lessons 1 and 6, you have an in-class presentation, so you don't have a reading assignment. To complete the workbook, read the slides and listen closely to your instructor while you're answering the questions.

For the other lessons, each reading assignment in the text matches a lesson in the Student Workbook. These lessons in the Workbook have the following parts:

PART A has key terms from the text with space for your written definition. You may have to revisit the text to define all the terms.

PART B asks you to Fill in the Blanks with one word in each blank. You can check the text for the exact words to use in the blanks. Occasionally, you'll find that more than one word fits the blank. Usually, one word is a little better than the other and the text has the exact word to use.

PART C is Multiple Choice, so circle the answer that most correctly answers the question. Only one answer is correct for each question. All questions come from the sections in the text.

PART D is Matching. As the heading to this section states, match the item in column one with its description in column two. You may use each letter only once but you won't use all of them.

PART E is True or False. Place a T or F in the blank based on whether the statement is true or false. Referring to the text may help you decide.

PART F has the Short Answer questions. We left some space under each question for your answer.

PART G is a special List or Describe section. These questions are meant to make you think and apply the text material. You can discuss your ideas with your instructor and classmates.

So that covers the Workbook. We hope you enjoy *Explorations*. We know you'll learn and remember things from the course better if you work through all the questions in this Workbook.

Lesson 1 The Cosmic Landscape
(Reading: None. In-class presentation only.)

The Cosmic Landscape

1. Define astronomy

2. Earth and _____ other planets orbit our Sun.

3. The planet _____ is closest to our Sun.
    a. Mercury
    b. Venus
    c. Jupiter
    d. Pluto

4. _____ is the largest planet orbiting our Sun.
    a. Venus
    b. Earth
    c. Jupiter
    d. Saturn

5. _____ True or False: Neptune is a planet in our solar system.

6. Our Sun is a huge ball of _____ that is _____ times more massive than Earth.

7. If our Sun were the size of a volleyball, Earth would be about the size of a _____, and Jupiter would be about the size of a _____.
    a. Button, dime
    b. Pinhead, nickel
    c. Dime, quarter
    d. Golf ball, baseball

8. Smaller bodies, such as _____, are part of our solar system.
    a. Moons
    b. Asteroids
    c. Comets
    d. All of the above

The Cosmic Landscape

9. Define solar system

10. Define light speed

11. A light year is the _____ light travels in one _____ .

    a. Time, year

    b. Speed, second

    c. Distance, second

    d. Distance, year

12. How can we measure huge distances in the universe?

13. When we combine all the local superclusters, we have the _____ _____ .

14. The distance from the Sun to Earth is about _____ miles.

15. Our solar system is a tiny part of the galaxy called the _____ _____ .

16. Our galaxy is one of 30 galaxies that form the _____ _____ of galaxies.

    a. Local Group

    b. Local Community

    c. Great Band

    d. Great Group

17. _____ True or False: Our Local Supercluster is about 50 million light years across.

18. Define gravity

19. _____ holds Earth in orbit around the Sun.

    a. Magnetism

    b. Gravity

    c. String

    d. Radiation

20. _____ True or False: We don't know what force holds our Sun in orbit around the center of the Milky Way galaxy.

The Cosmic Landscape

2. Why have constellation star patterns stayed the same for many hundreds of years?

G. List or Describe:

1. Describe how we see seasonal changes in the constellations.

Lesson 3 Prehistoric Astronomy, Part 2
(Reading: Section 1.1, pp. 14-16)

Prehistoric Astronomy, Part 2

A. Define, Describe, or Identify:

None

B. Fill in the Blanks:

Fill in the blank with the word or words needed to complete the statement.

1. Similar to prehistoric people, we can observe the _____ of the Moon.

2. The Moon's appearance changes slightly every day and takes about _____ days to go through a cycle.

3. When the Moon's fully lit surface faces Earth, we see a _____ Moon.

4. When 1/4 of the Moon's lit surface faces Earth, and the lit part is growing, we call it a _____ _____ Moon.

C. Multiple Choice:

Circle the letter that correctly answers the question or completes the statement.

1. We explain the Moon's phases by looking at the relative positions of the _____.

     a. Sun

     b. Moon

     c. Earth

     d. All of the above

2. The Moon rises about _____ minutes later every day during its cycle.

     a. 10

     b. 20

     c. 30

     d. 50

3. When ¾ of the Moon's lit surface faces the Earth, and the lit part is shrinking, we say it's a _____ _____ Moon.

    a. First quarter

    b. Waxing Gibbous

    c. Waning Gibbous

    d. Third quarter

4. A full Moon is visible only during _____ on Earth.

    a. Darkness

    b. Daylight

    c. Winter

    d. Twilight

D. Matching:

Match the term in Column A with the description in Column B. Write the letter of your answer on the line before the term. You may use each item from Column B only once, but you won't use all of them.

Column A

1. ____ Month
2. ____ Moon's appearance
3. ____ New Moon
4. ____ Full Moon
5. ____ First quarter

Column B

a. Follows a 30-day cycle

b. Not visible

c. Between waxing crescent and waxing gibbous

d. Comes from the word moon

e. Returns to the same view in 40 days

f. Moon and Sun are on opposite sides of Earth

g. Between waning crescent and waning gibbous

E. True/False:

Place a **T** in the blank if the statement is true, and an **F** in the blank if the statement is false.

_____ 1. The Moon rises in the west and sets in the east.

_____ 2. The Sun always lights half the Moon.

_____ 3. The Moon's phases occur because we see different amounts of its lit surface.

F. Short Answer (Things to Think About):

Write a short answer to each question.

1. Why can't we see a new Moon on Earth?

G. List or Describe:

1. Describe how the Moon's phases work.

Lesson 4 Early Ideas of the Heavens: Classical Astronomy

(Reading: Section 1.2, pp. 18-24)

Early Ideas of the Heavens: Classical Astronomy

A. Define, Describe, or Identify:

1. Epicycles

2. Geocentric theory

B. Fill in the Blanks:

Fill in the blank with the word or words needed to complete the statement.

1. The first astronomers we know were from ancient _____ and _____. They lived between 500 B.C. and 150 A.D.

2. About 300 B.C., Aristotle used _____ _____ during a lunar eclipse to show that Earth was round.

3. Aristarchus estimated that the Sun was _____ times farther away from the Earth than the Moon, but he was wrong because the Sun is _____ times farther away.

4. Eratosthenes used simple _____ and _____ measurements to estimate accurately the Earth's circumference.

5. Some ancient astronomers saw that objects in the sky moved _____ to _____, so they assumed _____ was the center of the universe.

6. Eudoxus proposed a geometric model that showed each space object mounted on its own revolving transparent _____.

7. _____'s model predicted planetary motion very well.

C. Multiple Choice:

Circle the letter that correctly answers the question or completes the statement.

1. Using their eyes and simple math, ancient astronomers determined
   _____ _____.

   a. Earth's shape

   b. Earth's size

   c. Moon's size

   d. All of the above

2. Aristotle said Earth was round because a traveler moving south saw new stars that had been hidden below the _____ _____.

   a. Ocean waves

   b. Sun's disk

   c. Southern horizon

   d. All of the above

3. Aristarchus used Earth's shadow on the Moon during an eclipse to estimate that the Moon's diameter was about _____ as large as the Earth's.

   a. 1/2

   b. 1/3

   c. 1/4

   d. 1/5

4. Geocentric means _____ centered.

   a. Sun

   b. Moon

   c. Earth

   d. Geometry

5. About 150 A.D., Ptolemy improved on the geocentric model by using 80 _____ to describe the motion of the Sun, Moon, and five known planets.

   a. Circles

   b. Lines

   c. Spheres

   d. Curves

6. Scientists are applying _____ _____ when they choose a simple theory over a more complicated one.

   a. Ptolemy's theorem

   b. Aristotle's plan

   c. Eudoxus' image

   d. Occam's razor

D. Matching:

Match the term in Column A with the description in Column B. Write the letter of your answer on the line before the term. You may use each item from Column B only once, but you won't use all of them.

Column A

1. _____ Pythagorus
2. _____ Aristotle
3. _____ Aristarchus
4. _____ Eratosthenes
5. _____ Ptolemy
6. _____ William of Occam

Column B

a. Great spheres describe star motion

b. Simpler theories probably were better

c. Close estimate of the Moon's diameter

d. Epicycles predicted planetary motion well

e. Gods formed a perfectly round Earth

f. Earth is 25,000 miles around

g. Earth is round because its shadow on the Moon during eclipses is curved

h. Moon at the center of the universe

E. True/False:

Place a **T** in the blank if the statement is true, and an **F** in the blank if the statement is false.

_____ 1. Luckily for us, the ancient astronomers were always correct in their calculations and theories.

_____ 2. Aristarchus used a triangle to estimate the Earth-to-Sun distance when the Moon was exactly half lit.

_____ 3. Ptolemy's model accurately described the subtle motions of the Sun, stars, and planets.

_____ 4. Ptolemy's epicycle model eventually was too complicated to believe.

F. Short Answer (Things to Think About):

Write a short answer to each question.

1. What are two observations that ancient Greek astronomers used to make their calculations?

2. What is Occam's razor?

3. How did Aristotle determine Earth was round?

G. List or Describe:

1. Which of the ancient astronomers do you think contributed the most to astronomy?

Lesson 5 Astronomy in the Renaissance
(Reading: Section 1.3)

Astronomy in the Renaissance

A. Define, Describe, or Identify:

1. Ellipse

2. Heliocentric model

3. Retrograde motion

B. Fill in the Blanks:

Fill in the blank with the word or words needed to complete the statement.

1. Nicolaus Copernicus challenged earlier theories of the _____
    solar system, but many scientists and the church didn't accept his ideas.

2. _____ _____ occurs when the Earth and another
    planet pass each other in their orbits.

3. Tyco Brahe observed unusual space objects that suggested the heavens were more
    _____ and _____ than anyone had believed.

4. One of Kepler's laws states that planets don't move in circles but in
    _____ around the Sun.

5. _____ calculated exactly how long each planet takes to orbit around
    the Sun.

6. _____ _____ was the first person to use a
    telescope to study the heavens and offer opinions about what he saw.

C. Multiple Choice:

Circle the letter that correctly answers the question or completes the statement.

1. Nicolaus Copernicus believed in the _____ model of the solar system that came from Aristarchus.

    a. Geocentric

    b. Heliocentric

    c. Galaxy

    d. Greek

2. Copernicus calculated the distance from the _____ to the _____ with amazing accuracy.

    a. Moon, Earth

    b. Earth, Mars

    c. Planets, Sun

    d. All of the above

3. Tycho Brahe designed and built _____ better than any other yet made.

    a. Telescopes

    b. Models

    c. Observatories

    d. Instruments

4. Johannes Kepler used _____ observations to learn how to explain planetary motion.

    a. Galileo's

    b. Brahe's

    c. Aristarchus'

    d. Copernicus'

5. The closer a planet's orbit takes it to the Sun, the _____ it moves.

    a. Faster

    b. Slower

    c. Safer

    d. Smoother

6. The Sun has _____, so it isn't perfect. It changes appearance and rotates.

    a. Spots

    b. Mountains

    c. Oceans

    d. Clouds

D. Matching:

Match the term in Column A with the description in Column B. Write the letter of your answer on the line before the term. You may use each item from Column B only once, but you won't use all of them.

Column A	*Column B*
1. ____ Geocentric model	a. Sits at one focus of planetary ellipses
2. ____ Tyco Brahe	b. Planets follow elliptical orbits
3. ____ The Sun	c. Lost part of his ear in a sword fight
4. ____ Milky Way	d. Couldn't explain the planets' retrograde motion
5. ____ Galileo Galilei	e. The Moon is a ball of rock
	f. Accurate planet measurements
	g. Uncountable number of stars

E. True/False:

Place a **T** in the blank if the statement is true, and an **F** in the blank if the statement is false.

_____ 1. Tyco Brahe made amazing observations of space objects with his accurate instruments.

_____ 2. Copernicus couldn't explain the locations of the planets, so his theory was wrong, and he dropped it.

_____ 3. Although Brahe and Kepler lived at the same time, they never knew each other.

_____ 4. The farther a planet is from the Sun, the longer it takes to complete its orbit.

_____ 5. Galileo Galilei saw moons orbiting Jupiter, so he knew everything must not orbit Earth.

F. Short Answer (Things to Think About):

Write a short answer to each question.

1. What idea did Copernicus develop and promote?

2. What happened to Galileo Galilei when he announced findings from his telescopic observations of space objects?

G. List or Describe:

1. List Kepler's three laws of planetary motion.

Lesson 6 Backyard Astronomy

(Reading: None. In-class presentation only)

Backyard Astronomy

1. Define dark adaptation

2. The width of your index finger held at arm's length up to the sky is about
   _____ degrees.

   a. 2

   b. 4

   c. 10

   d. 20

3. _____ True or False: Your hand is about 10 degrees wide if held at arms length up
   to the sky.

4. _____ is the brightest star in the northern sky.

5. _____ True or False: Polaris is part of the Big Dipper.

6. How can you find the North Star?

7. In the night sky, stars move _____ to _____.

8. A time-lapsed photograph of Polaris shows it _____ while the
   other stars _____.

   a. Stationary, gyrate

   b. Stationary, rotate

   c. Rotate, twinkle

   d. Rotate, are fixed

9. _____ True or False: For centuries people have navigated by the North Star
   because it stays fixed above the North Pole.

10. An arrow from the _____ Pole through the _____ Pole points at Polaris, the North Star.

11. _____ True or False: Constellations don't change much over thousands of years, so we can connect with our past through their stories and lore.

12. Important collections of stars in the sky that aren't constellations are called _____.

    a. Moons

    b. Galaxies

    c. Asterisms

    d. Equinoxes

13. Altitude and azimuth are angles in the _____ coordinate system.

14. Define altitude

15. Define azimuth

16. Describe how to use the horizon coordinate system to locate a star.

17. _____ and _____ are easy to spot in the night sky even though they are small planets because they are so close to Earth.

    a. Pluto, Neptune

    b. Mercury, Venus

    c. Uranus, Mars

    d. Saturn, Uranus

Lesson 7 Earth as a Planet and the Earth's Interior
(Reading: Sections 2.1-2.2)

Earth as a Planet and the Earth's Interior

A. Define, Describe, or Identify:

1. Crust

2. Density

3. Differentiation

4. Inner core

5. Liquid core

6. Mantle

7. Outer core

8. Silicates

9. Solid core

B. Fill in the Blanks:

Fill in the blank with the word or words needed to complete the statement.

1. Earth is a huge, rocky _____, spinning in space and moving around the _____ to the tune of about _____ miles every few seconds.

2. The Earth's _____ shaped it into a sphere.

3. Silicon and oxygen usually occur in Earth's crust together as _____.

4. We learn about Earth's interior by studying _____ (waves) and Earth's _____.

5. Some earthquake waves go _____ through the Earth, helping scientists know more about the core material.

C. Multiple Choice:

Circle the letter that correctly answers the question or completes the statement.

1. Earth spins on its axis once every _____ hours.

   a. 4

   b. 24

   c. 48

   d. 72

2. An iron-magnesium silicate with an olive green color, found plentifully within Earth's interior, is _____.

   a. Quartz

   b. Sand

   c. Gold

   d. Olivine

3. _____ is a measure of how much matter is packed into a given space (volume).

   a. Density

   b. Inertia

   c. Composition

   d. Gravity

4. Ordinary surface rocks weigh about _____ per cubic centimeter.

   a. 1 gram

   b. 3 grams

   c. 5.5 grams

   d. None of the above

5. Earth's outer layer is the _____.

    a. Inner core

    b. Outer core

    c. Mantle

    d. Crust

6. Scientists believe the temperature of Earth's core is _____ K.

    a. 0

    b. 212

    c. 495. 7

    d. 6500

D. Matching:

Match the term in Column A with the description in Column B. Write the letter of your answer on the line before the term. You may use each item from Column B only once, but you won't use all of them.

Column A

1. _____ Density

2. _____ Earth

3. _____ Oblate spheroid

4. _____ Quartz

5. _____ Outer core

6. _____ Inner core

Column B

a. Bulged like water slopping over the sides of a spinning bowl

b. 12,800 km in diameter

c. Travels 100 miles per hour in its path

d. Thick solid made of iron and nickel

e. Measures how much matter is in a given space

f. 8 grams per cubic centimeter

g. This silicate is ordinary sand

h. Thick liquid made of iron and nickel

E. True/False:

Place a **T** in the blank if the statement is true, and an **F** in the blank if the statement is false.

_____ 1. Earth's average density is 5.5 grams per cubic centimeter.

_____ 2. We learn about Earth's interior by drilling deep holes in the surface: hundreds of kilometers into the crust.

_____ 3. Under Earth's crust is the mantle, which is made mostly of silicates.

_____ 4. Surface rocks are eight times denser than water.

_____ 5. From Earth's density and size we know it weighs 6×10^{21} (6,000,000,000,000,000,000,000) metric tons. That's 6 sextillion metric tons or 6×10^{27} grams.

F. Short Answer (Things to Think About):

Write a short answer to each question.

1. What events give scientists information on the Earth's interior? What do the scientists study about these events?

2. How did the Earth's interior layers form? Was the Earth liquid or solid when this process started?

G. List or Describe:

1. Describe the materials and conditions at the Earth's core. What processes probably cause these conditions?

Lesson 8 Motions in the Earth's Interior

(Reading: Section 2.4)

Motions in the Earth's Interior

A. Define, Describe, or Identify:

1. Convection

2. Earthquake

3. Plate tectonics

4. Rifting

5. Subduction

6. Volcano

B. Fill in the Blanks:

Fill in the blank with the word or words needed to complete the statement.

1. When we heat a liquid or gas, it becomes less _____ and _____.

2. During convection, the liquid on the surface cools, becomes more _____, and then _____.

3. High _____ within the Earth cause _____ in the mantle.

4. When heated, the solid rock within the Earth's _____ may move slowly.

5. During _____, old crust material is dragged to the side, making oceans wider.

C. Multiple Choice:

Circle the letter that correctly answers the question or completes the statement.

1. The motion of boiling water in a pot is an example of _____.
    a. Radiation
    b. Subduction
    c. A volcano
    d. Convection

2. During convection, hotter material becomes less _____ and begins to _____.
    a. Dense, rise
    b. Dense, sink
    c. Fluid, cool
    d. Fluid, solidify

3. _____ decay within Earth's core causes very high temperatures.
    a. Volcanic
    b. Decomposition
    c. Radioactive
    d. Subduction

4. When Earth's mantle and crust move, the force is strong enough to move _____.
    a. The core
    b. Continents
    c. The Moon
    d. None of the above

5. When hot material from Earth's mantle rises through the crust, it causes _____.
    a. Old crust to sink
    b. Earthquakes
    c. Volcanoes
    d. None of the above

6. During _____, old crust material sinks deep into the Earth's mantle.

    a. Volcanoes

    b. Subduction

    c. Rifting

    d. None of the above

D. Matching:

Match the term in Column A with the description in Column B. Write the letter of your answer on the line before the term. You may use each item from Column B only once, but you won't use all of them.

Column A

1. _____Convection

2. _____Rifting

3. _____Earthquake

4. _____Plate

5. _____Volcano

Column B

a. A break in Earth's crust

b. In hot soup, a lima bean rises here and a noodle sinks there

c. Atlantic Ocean plate

d. Makes oceans wider

e. Hot crust material returns to the surface after being forced into the mantle

f. Cool material rises to the surface

g. Solid section of Earth's surface that moves slowly

E. True/False:

Place a **T** in the blank if the statement is true, and an **F** in the blank if the statement is false.

_____ 1. Heating and cooling of a liquid or gas causes convection.

_____ 2. Convection within the Earth occurs only in the core.

_____ 3. Earthquakes and volcanoes happen because the solid material in Earth's mantle moves around.

_____ 4. Millions of years ago, the African and South American plates fit close together.

_____ 5. Rifting destroys the Earth's old crust.

F. Short Answer (Things to Think About):

Write a short answer to each question.

1. What is convection? List some common examples of convection.

2. Describe how rifting and subduction cause earthquakes and volcanoes.

G. List or Describe:

1. Describe what happens during plate tectonics.

Lesson 9 The Earth's Atmosphere
(Reading: Section 2.5)

The Earth's Atmosphere

A. Define, Describe, or Identify:

1. Atmosphere

2. Electromagnetic spectrum

3. Greenhouse effect

4. Infrared radiation

5. Ozone

6. Radiation

7. Ultraviolet

B. Fill in the Blanks:

Fill in the blank with the word or words needed to complete the statement.

1. Earth's _____ is the layer of gases that surround us and give us weather.

2. Our atmosphere protects us from harmful _____.

3. Our atmosphere contains _____% oxygen and _____% nitrogen.

4. Three _____ explain where Earth's atmosphere came from.

5. Millions of years ago, the atmosphere contained poisonous gases such as _____ and _____.

6. The Sun's light contains all the colors of the _____.

7. The _____ (O₃) layer shields us from harmful ultraviolet radiation.

C. Multiple Choice:

Circle the letter that correctly answers the question or completes the statement.

1. Earth's atmosphere gives us _____.

    a. Air

    b. Rain

    c. Heat

    d. All of the above

2. _____ _____ released gases locked within Earth's rocks.

    a. Violent earthquakes

    b. Volcanic eruptions

    c. Tidal waves

    d. Ozone layer

3. _____ released gases when they vaporized upon impact.

    a. Avalanches

    b. Asteroids

    c. Comets

    d. Moons

4. The Suns rays broke down poisonous gases into _____ and _____.

    a. Carbon, nitrogen

    b. Oxygen, nitrogen

    c. Methane, ammonia

    d. Argon, ozone

5. The rainbow of visible light is part of a full range of radiation called the _____ _____.

    a. Colored light

    b. Roy G Biv

    c. Electromagnetic spectrum

    d. Ultraviolet light

6. Sunlight contains colors we can't see, such as _____ and _____ light.

   a. Orange, red

   b. Ultraviolet, infrared

   c. Bright, invisible

   d. Indigo, violet

7. _____ light goes right through the atmosphere.

   a. Visible

   b. Ultraviolet

   c. Dark

   d. None of the above

D. Matching:

Match the term in Column A with the description in Column B. Write the letter of your answer on the line before the term. You may use each item from Column B only once, but you won't use all of them.

Column A

1. ____ Atmosphere

2. ____ Carbon dioxide

3. ____ Ancient plants

4. ____ Methane

5. ____ Infrared radiation

6. ____ Greenhouse effect

Column B

a. Water and carbon dioxide absorb heat near Earth's surface

b. Earth gives off its heat

c. Released trapped gases during impact

d. Same as heat

e. 600 kilometers (373 miles) thick

f. One of the gases in the atmosphere

g. Put oxygen in the atmosphere

h. Poisonous gas in the atmosphere in prehistoric times

E. True/False:

Place a **T** in the blank if the statement is true, and an **F** in the blank if the statement is false.

_____ 1. About 10% of Earth's atmosphere is ozone, water, carbon dioxide, and argon.

_____ 2. Asteroid impacts also released gases locked inside Earth's rocks.

_____ 3. Photosynthesis within plants created the oxygen in our atmosphere.

_____ 4. The ozone layer is 600 kilometers above Earth's surface.

_____ 5. The greenhouse effect raises the atmosphere's temperature too high for living organisms.

F. Short Answer (Things to Think About):

Write a short answer to each question.

1. List the theories that describe how Earth got its atmosphere.

2. What is the ozone (O_3) layer and how does it help us?

G. List or Describe:

1. Describe the greenhouse effect.

Lesson 10 The Earth's Magnetic Field

(Reading: Section 2.6)

The Earth's Magnetic Field

A. Define, Describe, or Identify:

1. Aurora

2. Magnetic field

3. Magnetic lines of force

4. Polarity

5. Van Allen radiation belts

B. Fill in the Blanks:

Fill in the blank with the word or words needed to complete the statement.

1. _____ fields are shown on a diagram by lines that start at one end and circle around to the other end.

2. The _____ the lines are, the stronger the magnetic field.

3. We say magnetic fields have _____, which is direction from one pole to the other.

4. Earth behaves like a giant _____ magnet, producing a magnetic field between its north and south magnetic poles.

5. _____ currents cause magnetic fields.

6. Earth's magnetic field _____ us against electrically charged particles coming from the Sun.

C. Multiple Choice:

Circle the letter that correctly answers the question or completes the statement.

1. Magnetic field lines point in the direction a (an) _____ _____ would point.

    a. Electrical current

    b. Magnetic compass

    c. North pole

    d. Space traveler

2. Electrical currents in the Earth occur in the _____ _____.

    a. Hot mantle

    b. Solid crust

    c. Iron core

    d. None of the above

3. Earth's magnetic poles change their _____ and _____ from year to year.

    a. Position, strength

    b. North, south

    c. Direction, shape

    d. Polarity, location

4. Iron filings sprinkled on a piece of paper that lies on a bar (toy) magnet act like a _____ _____ and align with the magnetic field.

    a. Solid crust

    b. Compass needle

    c. North pole

    d. None of the above

5. Earth's magnetic field occurs because of _____ _____ in the liquid iron core.

    a. Bar (toy) magnets

    b. Ocean currents

    c. Electrical currents

    d. None of the above

6. Earth's magnetic field _____ harmful particles so they flow around the Earth.

    a. Deflects

    b. Absorbs

    c. Reflects

    d. Attracts

D. Matching:

Match the term in Column A with the description in Column B. Write the letter of your answer on the line before the term. You may use each item from Column B only once, but you won't use all of them.

Column A

1. _____ Magnetic field

2. _____ Earth's magnetic field

3. _____ Earth's true north pole

4. _____ Solar charged particles

5. _____ Van Allen radiation belts

6. _____ Aurora

Column B

a. Absorbs light from excited charged particles

b. Comes from electrical currents in the core

c. Align with spacecraft in orbit

d. Light from oxygen and nitrogen molecules in the upper atmosphere

e. Imaginary lines that flow from north pole to south pole in magnets

f. Doughnut-shaped rings around the Earth

g. Deflected by Earth's magnetic field into a spiral motion

h. Different location from magnetic north pole

E. True/False:

Place a **T** in the blank if the statement is true, and an **F** in the blank if the statement is false.

_____ 1. Some magnets have only one magnetic pole.

_____ 2. Earth's magnetic poles align perfectly with its geographic poles.

_____ 3. Scientists think that Earth's magnetic field comes from electrical currents flowing with the core's rotation and convection.

_____ 4. Earth's magnetic poles reverse their polarity about every 10,000 years.

_____ 5. Two doughnut-shaped rings form the Van Allen radiation belts.

F. Short Answer (Things to Think About):

Write a short answer to each question.

1. What is a magnetic field?

2. Describe what causes Earth's magnetic field and how it protects us against harmful charged particles from the Sun.

G. List or Describe:

1. Describe how and where auroras form.

Lesson 11 Description and Structure of the Moon
(Reading: Sections 3.1-3.2)

Description and Structure of the Moon

A. Define, Describe, or Identify:

1. Crater

2. Highlands

3. Maria

4. Rays

5. Rilles

6. Vacuum

B. Fill in the Blanks:

Fill in the blank with the word or words needed to complete the statement.

1. The first people set foot on the Moon in the year _____ during the _____ Space Program.

2. The Moon's interior is nearly _____ because of its _____ size.

3. The Moon has less _____ material than the Earth does to supply internal heat.

4. Like Earth, the Moon has a _____ and a _____, as well as a core.

5. Because the Moon has a cold interior, low levels of iron and nickel, and a slow rotation, it has no _____ _____.

6. On the Moon's surface, we see two major regions, the _____ and the _____.

C. Multiple Choice:

Circle the letter that correctly answers the question or completes the statement.

1. The Moon is considered a "dead" world because it has no _____.
    a. Atmosphere
    b. Plate tectonics
    c. Volcanoes
    d. All of the above

2. Because the Moon is so small, it _____ much faster than Earth.
    a. Formed
    b. Cooled
    c. Spins
    d. Decays

3. Without a hot interior, _____ can't occur in the Moon's mantle.
    a. Radiation
    b. Rotation
    c. Convection
    d. None of the above

4. The Moon's mantle is too _____ and _____ for its core to stir it.
    a. Thick, fluid
    b. Thin, fluid
    c. Hot, rigid
    d. Cold, rigid

5. Because the Moon is small, its gravity isn't strong enough to hold a (n) _____.
    a. Rock
    b. Atmosphere
    c. Astronaut
    d. Crater

6. The Moon's surface gets very _____ during the day and very _____ at night.

    a. Hot, cold

    b. Wet, dry

    c. Windy, calm

    d. Cloudy, clear

7. The Moon's surface features include _____.

    a. Craters

    b. Rays

    c. Rilles

    d. All of the above

D. Matching:

Match the term in Column A with the description in Column B. Write the letter of your answer on the line before the term. You may use each item from Column B only once, but you won't use all of them.

Column A

1. _____ Moon's explorers

2. _____ Moon's core

3. _____ Highlands

4. _____ Craters

5. _____ Tectonic plates

6. _____ Rilles

Column B

a. Thin layer of powder

b. Lunar canyons

c. Caused by meteor impacts

d. Twelve astronauts set foot on the surface

e. Pitted with craters

f. Not on the Moon

g. Lacks much heat and iron or nickel, compared to Earth's

h. Giant volcanoes

E. True/False:

Place a **T** in the blank if the statement is true, and an **F** in the blank if the statement is false.

_____ 1. The Moon has about ½ the Earth's diameter.

_____ 2. The Moon's core has less iron and nickel than Earth's core.

_____ 3. Astronauts couldn't tell if the Moon has a magnetic field.

_____ 4. Astronauts found the Moon covered with a thick layer of rock chunks and powder.

_____ 5. Astronaut Aldrin described the Moon's surface as a "magnificent desolation."

F. Short Answer (Things to Think About):

Write a short answer to each question.

1. How is the Moon's interior different from the Earth's?

2. How did the Moon's size affect its internal heat?

3. Why doesn't the Moon have a magnetic field?

4. Why doesn't the Moon have an atmosphere?

G. List or Describe:

1. Describe the Moon's surface regions and features.

Lesson 12 The Moon's Motions and Influence on Tides
(Reading: Sections 3.3 and 3.6)

The Moon's Motions and Influence on Tides

A. Define, Describe, or Identify:

1. Neap tides

2. Spring tides

3. Tidal braking

4. Tidal bulge

5. Tides

B. Fill in the Blanks:

Fill in the blank with the word or words needed to complete the statement.

1. People first saw pictures of the back side of the Moon in the decade of the
    _____.

2. The Moon takes _____ days to orbit the Earth.

3. Earth's rotation underneath the Moon causes two _____ tides and two
    _____ tides a day on Earth.

4. Because of the tides, Earth's days get longer by about _____
    seconds every century.

C. Multiple Choice:

Circle the letter that correctly answers the question or completes the statement.

1. If Earth were the size of a baseball, the Moon would be the size of a _____.
   a. Pea
   b. Marble
   c. Quarter
   d. Baseball

2. The regular change in the height of the ocean's surface, we call _____.
   a. Waves
   b. Fishy
   c. Swells
   d. Tides

3. The Sun's _____ causes tides on the Earth, but it has less effect than the Moon.
   a. Light
   b. Particles
   c. Gravity
   d. Radiation

4. Tides cause the Moon to move _____ _____ every year.
   a. Closer in
   b. The same
   c. Farther away
   d. Upside down

D. Matching:

Match the term in Column A with the description in Column B. Write the letter of your answer on the line before the term. You may use each item from Column B only once, but you won't use all of them.

Column A

1. _____ 27.3 days
2. _____ High tides
3. _____ Spring tides
4. _____ Tidal braking

Column B

a. Slows Earth's rotation slightly

b. The Moon orbit period once around Earth

c. Sun's gravity partly cancels the Moon's gravity

d. Twice a year

e. Effect of the Sun's gravity adding to the Moon's gravity

f. Occurs twice a day

E. True/False:

Place a **T** in the blank if the statement is true, and an **F** in the blank if the statement is false.

_____ 1. The Moon's gravity pulls on Earth and causes the oceans to rise as they pass under the Moon.

_____ 2. People on Earth never see the Moon's dark side.

_____ 3. Neap tides are higher than normal tides.

_____ 4. The Moon moves 3 kilometers away from Earth each year.

F. Short Answer (Things to Think About):

Write a short answer to each question.

1. What causes the Moon to keep the same face toward Earth?

2. How does the Moon cause tides on Earth?

G. List or Describe:

1. Describe the Sun's effect on Earth's tides.

Lesson 13 Eclipses
(Reading: Section 3.5)

Eclipses

A. Define, Describe, or Identify:

1. Corona

2. Eclipse

3. Eclipse season

4. Lunar eclipse

5. Solar eclipse

B. Fill in the Blanks:

Fill in the blank with the word or words needed to complete the statement.

1. Seeing the Moon in the night sky has fueled human _____ throughout history.

2. The Moon's orbit around Earth _____ slightly compared to Earth's orbit around the Sun.

3. For a solar eclipse, the _____ comes between _____ and the Sun.

4. Eclipse seasons occur _____ a year.

5. The totally eclipsed Moon usually has a deep _____ color.

C. Multiple Choice:

Circle the letter that correctly answers the question or completes the statement.

1. A (An) _____ occurs when one astronomical body casts its shadow on another.

    a. Storm

    b. Earthquake

    c. Eclipse

    d. Collision

2. While Earth revolves around the Sun, the Moon is usually _____ or _____ Earth's orbit.

    a. Ahead, behind

    b. Above, below

    c. Faster, slower

    d. None of the above

3. The Moon's shadow _____ hits Earth.

    a. Rarely

    b. Monthly

    c. Yearly

    d. Constantly

4. Eclipses are visible in different _____ each time.

    a. Cities

    b. Communities

    c. Countries

    d. All of the above

5. A solar eclipse brings a short _____ in the middle of the _____.

    a. Day, night

    b. Night, day

    c. Storm, day

    d. Delay, night

D. Matching:

Match the term in Column A with the description in Column B. Write the letter of your answer on the line before the term. You may use each item from Column B only once, but you won't use all of them.

Column A

1. _____ Lunar eclipse
2. _____ Eclipse seasons
3. _____ Lunar orbit tilt
4. _____ Solar eclipse

Column B

a. The Sun's shadow falls on Earth

b. Animals awaken

c. Earth's shadow falls on the Moon

d. Makes the Moon's shadow miss Earth

e. Earth, Moon, and Sun align

f. Stars come out

E. True/False:

Place a **T** in the blank if the statement is true, and an **F** in the blank if the statement is false.

_____ 1. During a solar eclipse, Earth's shadow falls on the Moon.

_____ 2. The Moon's orbit tilts slightly compared to Earth's orbit around the Sun.

_____ 3. Earth's shadow covers part of the Moon every month.

_____ 4. When the Moon's orbit passes between Earth and the Sun, an eclipse might occur.

_____ 5. During a lunar eclipse, Earth's atmosphere scatters the red light, and the Moon looks a bright blue.

F. Short Answer (Things to Think About):

Write a short answer to each question.

1. When do eclipse seasons occur for Earth and the Moon? Does an eclipse occur during every season? Why or why not?

2. What causes the corona during a solar eclipse?

G. List or Describe:

1. Describe the difference between a solar eclipse and a lunar eclipse.

Lesson 14 Components of the Solar System
(Reading: p 94 and Section 4.1)

Components of the Solar System

A. Define, Describe, or Identify:

1. Asteroids

2. Asteroid belt

3. Astronomical unit (AU)

4. Comet

5. Differentiation

6. Jovian planets

7. Kuiper Belt

8. Oort cloud

9. Solar system

10. Terrestrial planets

B. Fill in the Blanks:

Fill in the blank with the word or words needed to complete the statement.

1. The solar system is our local _____ in space.

2. The Sun's _____ holds the solar system together.

3. All the planets follow _____ paths around the Sun.

4. All the planets travel _____ around the Sun, as viewed from above the Earth's North Pole.

5. _____ is the planet with its spin axis straight up (perpendicular to its orbital plane), and _____ is the planet with its spin axis almost upside down.

6. By studying how the planets move around the Sun, we can estimate their _____.

7. By knowing the average density of the inner planets (3.9 to 5.5 grams per cubic centimeter), we know they have a (an) _____ core.

8. The Moon is Earth's natural _____.

9. Comets are _____ bodies less than _____ kilometers across.

C. Multiple Choice:

Circle the letter that correctly answers the question or completes the statement.

1. Earth is one of _____ (known) planets in the solar system.

   a. five

   b. nine

   c. 13

   d. 15

2. The Sun has _____ times more mass than the rest of the solar system combined.

   a. 10

   b. 50

   c. 200

   d. 700

3. Compared to the rest of the planets, Jupiter is the _____.

    a. Smallest

    b. Largest

    c. Roundest

    d. Brightest

4. If Earth were the size of a baseball (10 centimeters), the Sun would be the size of a _____ that's _____ kilometer (s) away.

    a. Basketball, 0.5

    b. Car, 1

    c. Truck, 2

    d. House, 2

5. _____ and _____ appear to rotate on their sides.

    a. Mercury, Venus

    b. Mars, Jupiter

    c. Neptune, Uranus

    d. Uranus, Pluto

6. Knowing a planet's mass and size, we can estimate its _____.

    a. Spin

    b. Oceans

    c. Density

    d. Atmosphere

7. The Jovian planets have an average density of 0.71 to 1.67 grams per cubic centimeter, similar to that of _____.

    a. Ice

    b. Air

    c. Iron

    d. Mountains

8. Jupiter has the most natural satellites with _____.

    a. 10

    b. 39

    c. 63

    d. 101

9. Asteroids can be as big as _____ kilometers across.

    a. 10

    b. 100

    c. 1000

    d. 10,000

10. Comets orbit the Sun in the _____ _____ far beyond Pluto.

    a. Asteroid belt

    b. Inner belt

    c. Outer belt

    d. Oort cloud

D. Matching:

Match the term in Column A with the description in Column B. Write the letter of your answer on the line before the term. You may use each item from Column B only once, but you won't use all of them.

Column A

1. _____ The Sun
2. _____ Astronomical unit
3. _____ Inner planets
4. _____ Jovian planets
5. _____ Pluto
6. _____ 3.9 to 5.5 grams per cubic centimeter
7. _____ Mercury
8. _____ Comet

Column B

a. Terrestrial planets

b. Lack a well-defined surface

c. 71% hydrogen and 27% helium

d. Average density of the inner planets

e. No natural satellites

f. Grows a long tail as it approaches the Sun

g. May be the failed building blocks of a planet

h. Farthest planet

i. 150 million kilometers

j. Orbit tilts 17° from those of the rest of the planets

E. True/False:

Place a **T** in the blank if the statement is true, and an **F** in the blank if the statement is false.

_____ 1. The solar system contains just the Sun and its planets.

_____ 2. The diameter of the solar system is about 80 AU (12 billion kilometers).

_____ 3. Except for Pluto, all the planets lie in the same plane.

_____ 4. The inner planets all have rocky surfaces with thick cloudy atmospheres.

_____ 5. The Jovian planets have Earth-sized rocky cores.

_____ 6. The asteroid belt lies between Jupiter and Saturn.

F. Short Answer (Things to Think About):

Write a short answer to each question.

1. How do we know what a planet has inside of it?

2. How do scientists estimate the age of the solar system?

3. Where do we find comets?

G. List or Describe:

1. Describe what we know about the Sun.

Lesson 15 Origin of the Solar System and Other Planetary Systems
(Reading: Sections 4.2-4.3)

Origin of the Solar System and Other Planetary Systems

A. Define, Describe, or Identify:

1. Accretion

2. Condense

3. Interstellar cloud

4. Interstellar grains

5. Planetesimal

6. Solar nebula

7. Solar nebula hypothesis

B. Fill in the Blanks:

Fill in the blank with the word or words needed to complete the statement.

1. One of our deepest questions is, "How did our solar system _____?"

2. Theories of where our solar system came from depend on many _____ of the planets and the stars, plus complex computer modeling.

3. A _____ is a proposed explanation for a set of scientific observations.

4. Some astronomers think the solar system evolved from a rotating flattened disk made of _____ and _____.

5. Interstellar grains are a combination of _____, _____
   and _____ compounds, and _____ _____.

6. In the solar nebula that formed our solar system, the bulge became the
   _____ and the disk became the _____.

7. _____ occurs when a gas cools to a low enough temperature so
   its molecules stick together to form liquid or solid particles.

8. When smaller particles stick together to form larger particles, we call it
   _____.

9. Over time, _____ gently collided to form planets.

C. Multiple Choice:

Circle the letter that correctly answers the question or completes the statement.

1. Recently, astronomers have developed ways to detect _____ around
   other stars.
   a. Rings
   b. Planets
   c. Stars
   d. Moons

2. The current favorite explanation for the solar system's origin is the
   _____ _____ hypothesis.
   a. Rotating disk
   b. Gathering dust
   c. Solar nebula
   d. Bright star

3. Interstellar clouds are vast collections of _____.
   a. Gases
   b. Vapor
   c. Planets
   d. Stars

4. The interstellar cloud that formed our solar system probably was
   _____ astronomical units (AU) across and had
   _____ times our Sun's mass.

   a. 10, 10

   b. 90, 4

   c. 200, 2

   d. 350, 1

5. The solar nebula hypothesis says that it took several _____
   years to form the rotating disk with a bulge in the center.

   a. Hundred

   b. Thousand

   c. Million

   d. Billion

6. Before the planets formed, the inner part of the rotating disk was
   _____ and the outer part was _____.

   a. Moving, stationary

   b. Thin, thick

   c. Cold, hot

   d. Hot, cold

7. In step 2 of the solar nebula hypothesis, close to the Sun the temperature was too
   hot to form solid icy particles, but solid _____-
   _____ particles formed.

   a. Iron, ore

   b. Rocky, iron

   c. Hydrogen, helium

   d. Rocky mountains

8. In step 5 of the solar nebula hypothesis, larger objects (bigger than Earth) used
   their strong gravity to capture light _____.

   a. Gases

   b. Planets

   c. Moons

   d. Iron

9. Knowing that our galaxy had billions of stars, astronomers naturally wondered if we were the only solar system with _____.

    a. Asteroids

    b. Comets

    c. Planets

    d. None of the above

D. Matching:

Match the term in Column A with the description in Column B. Write the letter of your answer on the line before the term. You may use each item from Column B only once, but you won't use all of them.

Column A	Column B
1. _____ Interstellar cloud	a. Accretion
2. _____ Solar nebula	b. Outer disk formed icy and rocky-iron particles
3. _____ Step 2	c. Outer part became the Sun
4. _____ Step 3	d. On some inner planets by volcanic activity
5. _____ Planetesimals	e. Not enough gravity to hold an atmosphere
6. _____ Atmosphere formation	f. 200 astronomical units (AU) across and 10 AU thick
7. _____ Mercury	g. Radiation
	h. Beginning of our solar system 4.5 billion years ago
	i. Condensation

E. True/False:

Place a **T** in the blank if the statement is true, and an **F** in the blank if the statement is false.

_____ 1. Astronomers are discovering other solar systems every year.

_____ 2. Scientists use six steps to describe how the solar system formed.

_____ 3. Step one in the solar nebula hypothesis says an solar nebula collapsed into an interstellar cloud.

_____ 4. The solar nebula hypothesis says that, during step 4, large particles collided and stuck together, forming planetesimals.

_____ 5. During step 6, continuing collisions of planetesimals and internal radioactivity melted the planets.

_____ 6. Often astronomers find Jupiter-sized and Earth-sized planets around other stars in our galaxy.

F. Short Answer (Things to Think About):

Write a short answer to each question.

1. Any good theory about how our solar system formed must answer what key questions?

2. How did astronomers discover that other stars had planets in orbit around them?

3. What happened in the final step of our solar system's formation?

G. List or Describe:

1. Describe the difference between how the inner and outer parts of the solar system formed.

Lesson 16 The Terrestrial Planets and Mercury
(Reading: Sections 5.1-5.2)

The Terrestrial Planets and Mercury

A. Define, Describe, or Identify:

None

B. Fill in the Blanks:

Fill in the blank with the word or words needed to complete the statement.

1. The _____ planets are the ones in the solar system most like Earth.

2. Mercury looks much like our _____ (gray, bare, and cratered), with almost no _____.

3. Venus is covered with thick _____ _____ clouds in a dense _____ _____ atmosphere.

4. Mars has a thin _____ _____ atmosphere.

5. Mercury's biggest crater is _____ _____, which is 1300 kilometers (about 800 miles) in diameter.

6. As Mercury cooled, it shrank like a dried apple, which created _____.

7. Mercury rotates on its axis exactly _____ times for every _____ trips around the Sun.

C. Multiple Choice:

Circle the letter that correctly answers the question or completes the statement.

1. The four terrestrial planets have similar _____ and _____.

    a. Colors, atmospheres

    b. Mountains, plains

    c. Sizes, structures

    d. Rotations, oceans

2. The inner planets are too small and too warm to capture _____ atmospheres similar to the giant gas planets.

    a. Cloudy

    b. Hydrogen

    c. Watery

    d. Oxygen

3. On Mercury, _____ flowed into many of its craters and across much of its surface.

    a. Lava

    b. Water

    c. Acid

    d. Clouds

4. Mercury shows no signs of _____.

    a. Craters

    b. Scarps (cliffs)

    c. Volcanoes

    d. Lava

5. Mercury's _____ magnetic field comes from its _____ mass and _____ rotation rate.

    a. Weak, large, fast

    b. Weak, small, slow

    c. Strong, large, slow

    d. Strong, small, fast

D. Matching:

Match the term in Column A with the description in Column B. Write the letter of your answer on the line before the term. You may use each item from Column B only once, but you won't use all of them.

Column A

1. ____ Moons among terrestrial planets
2. ____ Venus
3. ____ 800 and -280
4. ____ Mercury's solar day
5. ____ Mercury's magnetic field

Column B

a. Days in Mercury's year

b. Strong

c. Venus has three; Earth has one

d. 176 Earth days

e. Mercury's day and night Fahrenheit temperatures

f. Hotter surface than Mercury's

g. Earth has one; Mars has two

h. Weak

E. True/False:

Place a **T** in the blank if the statement is true, and an **F** in the blank if the statement is false.

_____ 1. Earth is a terrestrial planet with blue seas, white clouds, ice caps, red deserts, and green jungles.

_____ 2. Mercury's temperatures are among the hottest and coldest on any surface in the solar system.

_____ 3. Mercury has a low-density interior, made of iron and silicates.

_____ 4. A solar day (from one sunrise to the next one) on Mercury is about twice as long as its year.

_____ 5. On Mercury, you can see the sun set in the west, then rise again immediately in the west, then set again.

F. Short Answer (Things to Think About):

Write a short answer to each question.

1. What might have caused Mercury's thin silicate crust?

2. What prevented Mercury from forming an atmosphere?

G. List or Describe:

1. Describe what happens because of Mercury's long rotation rate and short time to orbit the Sun.

Lesson 17 Venus
(Reading: Section 5.3)

Venus

A. Define, Describe, or Identify:

1. Greenhouse effect

B. Fill in the Blanks:

Fill in the blank with the word or words needed to complete the statement.

1. Venus has a mass and diameter very close to _____.

2. Venus's clouds are very _____ and _____.

3. The _____ _____ occurs when atmospheric gases absorb heat and then trap it in the atmosphere, thus raising the temperature.

4. The Magellan spacecraft took _____ images of Venus's surface from above the atmosphere.

5. Venus's surface has mostly _____, gently _____ plains.

6. The volcanic landforms on Venus show _____-_____ domes of uplifted rock.

7. Scientists believe that Venus's surface is much _____ than Earth's

C. Multiple Choice:

Circle the letter that correctly answers the question or completes the statement.

1. Venus and Earth have very different _____ and
    _____.

    a. · Rings, moons

    b. Surfaces, atmospheres

    c. Sizes, masses

    d. Interiors, cores

2. Venus's atmospheric pressure is _____ times that of Earth's.

    a. 2

    b. 10

    c. 55

    d. 100

3. On Venus, the greenhouse effect is very strong because of the large amount of
    _____ _____ in the atmosphere.

    a. Sulphuric acid

    b. Carbon dioxide

    c. Nitrous oxide

    d. Oxygen molecules

4. A photograph from Russia's Venera spacecraft on the surface of Venus shows
    _____ _____ rocks.

    a. Flat, broken

    b. Round, large

    c. Red, dusty

    d. Small, cracked

5. Venus's surface has huge _____ flows from _____.

    a. Water, oceans

    b. Water, rivers

    c. Rocky, landslides

    d. Lava, volcanoes

6. The present surface of Venus is no more than _____ billion years old.

   a. A quarter of a

   b. Half a

   c. 4.5

   d. 10

7. Venus's interior is probably similar to Earth's, with a (an) _____ core and _____ mantle.

   a. Iron, liquid

   b. Liquid, nickel

   c. Iron, rock

   d. Solid, hot

D. Matching:

Match the term in Column A with the description in Column B. Write the letter of your answer on the line before the term. You may use each item from Column B only once, but you won't use all of them.

Column A	Column B
1. _____ Venus's clouds	a. Days of sunshine on Venus
2. _____ 900	b. Thin, wispy water vapor
3. _____ On Venus's surface	c. One rotation for Venus
4. _____ 243 Earth days	d. Venus rotates backward from Earth
5. _____ Sunrise in the west	e. Contain sulfuric acid droplets
	f. Fahrenheit temperature near Venus's surface
	g. Long narrow faults (cracks)

E. True/False:

Place a **T** in the blank if the statement is true, and an **F** in the blank if the statement is false.

_____ 1. Venus's atmosphere is 96% oxygen.

_____ 2. Because so much sunlight gets to Venus's surface, spacecraft have taken great photographs of the surface features.

_____ 3. Spacecraft have never landed on Venus.

_____ 4. Blue light is absorbed in Venus's atmosphere, so photographs of the surface appear orange.

_____ 5. On Venus, some volcanic lava flows look fresh.

F. Short Answer (Things to Think About):

Write a short answer to each question.

1. What is peculiar about Venus's rotation?

2. What evidence do we have that volcanic eruptions on Venus are recent?

G. List or Describe:

1. Describe two ideas that might explain the differences in the surfaces of Earth and Venus.

Lesson 18 Mars

(Reading: Sections 5.4 and 5.6)

Mars

A. Define, Describe, or Identify:

None

B. Fill in the Blanks:

Fill in the blank with the word or words needed to complete the statement.

1. Ancient observers named Mars after the Roman god of _____.

2. On Mars the sky is clear enough so we can see its _____ from Earth.

3. In 1971, _____ became the first satellite from Earth to orbit another planet—Mars.

4. After 20 years of no spacecraft going to Mars, the Mars _____ _____ and the Mars _____ reopened the book on the red planet.

5. Mars has _____ similar to Earth, so we can see its polar ice caps change size during the year.

6. At the mid-latitudes, Mars has vast uplands, called the _____ bulge, that are dotted with volcanic peaks.

7. Mars' low gravity and low volcanic activity probably caused it to lose its _____ during the first 1-2 billion years after it formed.

8. Mars has two moons named _____ and _____.

C. Multiple Choice:

Circle the letter that correctly answers the question or completes the statement.

1. Mars has a diameter _____ that of Earth's and a mass _____ that of Earth's.

    a. 1/3, 1/5

    b. 1/2, 1/10

    c. 1/10, 1/50

    d. 1/20, 1/50

2. For decades, blurred images of _____ _____ and dark lines that looked like _____ made people think of Martians.

    a. Ice caps, canals

    b. Large valleys, roads

    c. Deep canyons, pathways

    d. High mountains, tunnels

3. Recently, the twin Mars Exploration Rovers, named _____ and _____, roamed the Martian surface exploring its features.

    a. Mariner, Magellan

    b. Pioneer, Voyager

    c. Viking, Pathfinder

    d. Spirit, Opportunity

4. Mars' southern ice cap is made of _____ _____.

    a. Carbon dioxide

    b. Frozen water

    c. Icy dust

    d. None of the above

5. One volcanic peak, called _____ _____, rises 25 kilometers above the surface—three times taller than Mount Everest, the tallest peak on Earth.

    a. Mount Olympus

    b. Valles Marineris

    c. Olympus Mons

    d. Mount Whitney

6. Nighttime temperatures on Mars reach _____°F.

    a. -10

    b. -33

    c. -67

    d. −100

7. Despite clouds on Mars, no _____ falls.

    a. Rain

    b. Snow

    c. Dust

    d. All of the above

8. Scientists believe Mars' interior is differentiated like Earth's, so it has a _____.

    a. Crust

    b. Mantle

    c. Iron core

    d. All of the above

D. Matching:

Match the term in Column A with the description in Column B. Write the letter of your answer on the line before the term. You may use each item from Column B only once, but you won't use all of them.

Column A

1. ____ 50°F

2. ____ Mariner 4

3. ____ Valles Marineris

4. ____ Mars' northern ice cap

5. ____ Martian atmosphere

Column B

a. First satellite to orbit another planet

b. Water ice covered with dry ice

c. 95% oxygen

d. 1% of Earth's atmospheric density

e. Largest canyon in the solar system

f. A warm day on Mars

g. First close-up images of another planet

h. Low temperature on Mars

E. True/False:

Place a **T** in the blank if the statement is true, and an **F** in the blank if the statement is false.

_____ 1. The former Soviet Union and the United States launched unsuccessful missions to Mars.

_____ 2. The Earth's Grand Canyon is slightly longer, wider, and deeper than the Valles Marineris.

_____ 3. Bordering the Martian pole caps are vast deserts where strong winds blow dunes into parallel ridges.

_____ 4. Mars is odd for having mostly north-south winds.

_____ 5. Dry river beds on Mars show that liquid water flowed at one time.

_____ 6. Mars has no magnetic field, suggesting that its iron core is no longer liquid.

F. Short Answer (Things to Think About):

Write a short answer to each question.

1. What were the first two satellites to land on Mars and what was their mission?

2. What are some interesting features on the Mars surface?

G. List or Describe:

1. Describe some of the surface features that make astronomers think water once flowed on Mars.

Lesson 19 The Outer Planets and Jupiter

(Reading: Chapter 6 Introduction and Section 6.1, pp. 150-158)

The Outer Planets and Jupiter

A. Define, Describe, or Identify:

None

B. Fill in the Blanks:

Fill in the blank with the word or words needed to complete the statement.

1. The outer planets are _____, _____, _____, _____, and _____.

2. The outer planets are typically _____ in diameter; are made of _____, _____, or _____; lack a solid _____; and have cores of molten _____.

3. Jupiter is the largest planet in our solar system, with a diameter more than _____ times bigger than Earth's and a mass _____ times bigger than Earth's.

4. Although Jupiter contains mostly light elements, its large size and mass give it very strong _____.

5. Jupiter rotates at a high rate, creating the strongest _____ _____ in the solar system.

6. Scientists didn't know Jupiter had a _____ until the _____ spacecraft photographed it in 1979.

C. Multiple Choice:

Circle the letter that correctly answers the question or completes the statement.

1. _____ is the outer planet that is most different from the others.

   a. Saturn

   b. Uranus

   c. Neptune

   d. Pluto

2. Jupiter has dense, richly colored, parallel _____ bands that cloak the planet in secrecy.

   a. Mountain

   b. Wind

   c. Cloud

   d. Storm

3. Jupiter's average density is _____ grams per cubic centimeter, which is closer to water (1.0 gram per cubic centimeter) than to iron (8.0 grams per cubic centimeter).

   a. 0.7

   b. 1.3

   c. 2.5

   d. 3.1

4. Jupiter's _____ patterns and high _____ rate create powerful jet streams in its cloud belts.

   a. Cloud, wind

   b. Radiation, volcano

   c. Convection, rotation

   d. Subduction, rotation

5. Jupiter has the most moons of any planet in the solar system with _____.

   a. 8

   b. 19

   c. 27

   d. 39

6. _____ was first observer to see Jupiter's moons named Ganymede, Callisto, Io, and Europa.

    a. Brahe

    b. Copernicus

    c. Galileo

    d. Herschel

D. Matching:

Match the term in Column A with the description in Column B. Write the letter of your answer on the line before the term. You may use each item from Column B only once, but you won't use all of them.

Column A

1. ____ Jupiter's rotation rate

2. ____ 30,000 K

3. ____ Great Red Spot

4. ____ Ganymede

5. ____ Callisto

Column B

a. A cloud swirl between wind streams

b. Largest moon in the solar system

c. May have water underneath its icy surface

d. Once every 10 hours

e. Smallest moon around Jupiter

f. The Sun's surface temperature

g. Jupiter's core temperature

E. True/False:

Place a **T** in the blank if the statement is true, and an **F** in the blank if the statement is false.

_____ 1. Jupiter's atmosphere is mainly hydrogen, helium, methane, ammonia, and water.

_____ 2. Jupiter's strong gravity compresses gaseous hydrogen into a vast sea of liquid hydrogen below the clouds.

_____ 3. Jupiter's magnetic field creates auroras similar to those on Earth.

_____ 4. Ganymede and Callisto are moons that look like Earth's moon—cratered and covered in rock.

_____ 5. Europa has active volcanoes spouting sulfur out their tops.

F. Short Answer (Things to Think About):

Write a short answer to each question.

1. How does Jupiter's interior keep hydrogen in three different states (solid, liquid, and gas)?

2. What are the characteristics of Jupiter's four largest moons?

G. List or Describe:

1. Describe Jupiter's atmosphere.

Lesson 20 Saturn
(Reading: Section 6.2)

Saturn

A. Define, Describe, or Identify:

1. Roche limit

B. Fill in the Blanks:

Fill in the blank with the word or words needed to complete the statement.

1. Saturn is the _____ largest planet in the solar system, with a diameter that is _____ times larger than Earth's and a mass that's _____ times larger than Earth's.

2. Just outside Saturn's core is a layer of _____ _____.

3. Saturn's atmosphere prevents us from seeing underneath because of frozen _____ clouds.

4. Saturn's rings aren't solid, but are individual bodies made of _____, _____, and _____ compounds.

5. The pieces in Saturn's rings probably came from _____, _____, and _____ that came too close and broke apart.

6. Most of Saturn's moons are covered with _____ and surrounded by white markings of shattered _____.

C. Multiple Choice:

Circle the letter that correctly answers the question or completes the statement.

1. Saturn's average density is _____ grams per cubic centimeter, which means it must be made mostly of _____ and its compounds.

    a. 0.7, hydrogen

    b. 1.0, water

    c. 1.5, helium

    d. 2.3, methane

2. Saturn's core is made of _____.

    a. Rock

    b. Iron

    c. Water

    d. All of the above

3. Saturn's rings extend from about _____ kilometers to about _____ kilometers.

    a. 1000, 5000

    b. 5000, 20,000

    c. 30,000, 136,000

    d. 50,000, 300,000

4. A planet's gravity pulls on a satellite's _____ side more than its _____ side, which stretches it and can pull it apart.

    a. Far, near

    b. Near, far

    c. Dark, light

    d. Top, bottom

5. Most of Saturn's moons form a small _____ _____ with Saturn at the center.

    a. Moon colony

    b. Auxiliary ring

    c. Solar system

    d. None of the above

6. _____ is Saturn's largest moon and is bigger than
   _____.

    a. Mimas, Pluto

    b. Enceladus, Mercury

    c. Titan, Mercury

    d. Titan, Earth

D. Matching:

Match the term in Column A with the description in Column B. Write the letter of your answer on the line before the term. You may use each item from Column B only once, but you won't use all of them.

Column A

1. ____ Liquid helium droplets
2. ____ Roche limit
3. ____ Saturn's moons
4. ____ Titan

Column B

a. Mostly icy interiors

b. 1.22 times the planet's diameter

c. More dense than Jupiter's moons

d. 2.44 times the planet's radius

e. Inside Saturn's hydrogen layers

f. Clouds of methane or ethane

E. True/False:

Place a **T** in the blank if the statement is true, and an **F** in the blank if the statement is false.

_____ 1. The upper layers of Saturn's interior are helium.

_____ 2. Saturn's rings are more than a kilometer thick.

_____ 3. Standing on Titan would be like standing in a very cold gasoline (hydrocarbon ethane) rain.

_____ 4. All planetary rings lie near their planet's Roche limit.

_____ 5. Astronomers see Saturn's rings as smooth and uniform without gaps.

F. Short Answer (Things to Think About):

Write a short answer to each question.

1. List the four layers of Saturn's interior.

2. What are some characteristics of Saturn's atmosphere?

G. List or Describe:

1. Describe how Saturn's rings formed.

Lesson 21 Uranus, Neptune, and Pluto
(Reading: Sections 6.3-6.5)

Uranus, Neptune, and Pluto

A. Define, Describe, or Identify:

None

B. Fill in the Blanks:

Fill in the blank with the word or words needed to complete the statement.

1. _____, _____, and _____ are so far from the Sun that astronomers aren't sure of their makeup or how they or their moons formed.

2. Even with close-up images from the spacecraft _____, we see Uranus as nearly featureless.

3. Uranus has a density of _____ grams per cubic centimeter, so its interior must contain no more than just a core of rock and iron.

4. Uranus has _____ large moons and several small ones, consisting of rock and water and covered in craters.

5. During part of its year, Uranus alternates night and day in a _____-hour cycle.

6. Neptune's interior has a (n) _____ and _____ core surrounded by _____.

7. Pluto was discovered in _____. Its moon, Charon, was discovered in _____.

8. Pluto has _____ the diameter of Earth and an estimated density of _____ grams per cubic centimeter.

C. Multiple Choice:

Circle the letter that correctly answers the question or completes the statement.

1. Scientists suspect Uranus and Neptune, have a (n) _____ and _____ core with water in the interior.

   a. Hydrogen, helium

   b. Rock, iron

   c. Methane, ice

   d. None of the above

2. Uranus is smaller than Saturn but _____ times larger in diameter than Earth and with _____ times Earth's mass.

   a. 2, 10

   b. 4, 6

   c. 4, 15

   d. 6, 25

3. Uranus looks blue to us because the _____ gas in the atmosphere absorbs red light and leaves the blue light.

   a. Helium

   b. Hydrogen

   c. Ethane

   d. Methane

4. Uranus tilts _____ degrees, which suggests that something hit the planet while it was forming and knocked it on its side.

   a. About 90

   b. About 45

   c. About 30

   d. About 10

5. Uneven _____ may explain why Uranus doesn't have cloud bands similar to those around Saturn and Jupiter.

   a. Rotation

   b. Sunlight

   c. Water

   d. Heating

6. Neptune had a dark blue _____ that recently disappeared for unknown reasons.

    a. Spot

    b. Mountain

    c. Ocean

    d. Band

7. Neptune has _____ small, close moons and _____ moons farther out.

    a. 2, 4

    b. 4, 3

    c. 6, 2

    d. 5, 5

8. What we know about Pluto comes mostly from studying how _____ moves around it.

    a. Triton

    b. Charon

    c. Miranda

    d. Neptune

9. Pluto has a thin atmosphere of _____, _____ _____, and traces of _____.

    a. Nitrogen, carbon monoxide, methane

    b. Hydrogen, carbon dioxide, ethane

    c. Helium, water vapor, hydrogen

    d. Hydrogen, its compounds, methane

D. Matching:

Match the term in Column A with the description in Column B. Write the letter of your answer on the line before the term. You may use each item from Column B only once, but you won't use all of them.

Column A

1. _____ Sir William Herschel
2. _____ Uranus
3. _____ Uranus's atmosphere
4. _____ Miranda
5. _____ Neptune
6. _____ Triton

Column B

a. Oxygen and nitrogen

b. Discovered Neptune

c. Orbits Neptune backward

d. Disappearing rings

e. 19 astronomical units from the Sun

f. Uranus's moon that broke apart and then reformed

g. Discovered Uranus in 1781

h. Hydrogen and methane

E. True/False:

Place a **T** in the blank if the statement is true, and an **F** in the blank if the statement is false.

_____ 1. Because Uranus rotates moderately fast, its equator bulges.

_____ 2. Scientists found no evidence of rings around Uranus.

_____ 3. Uranus's tilt means it has an unusual day-night pattern during its year.

_____ 4. Neptune is much smaller than Uranus.

_____ 5. Unlike Uranus, Neptune has cloud belts.

_____ 6. Triton is large enough to support an atmosphere.

F. Short Answer (Things to Think About):

Write a short answer to each question.

1. How are the three outer planets similar? Different?

2. What's odd about Pluto's orbit around the Sun?

G. List or Describe:

1. Describe the day-night pattern on Uranus during its orbit around the Sun.

Glossary

absorption the process in which light or other electromagnetic radiation gives up its energy to an atom or molecule. For example, ozone in our atmosphere absorbs ultraviolet radiation.

absorption-line spectrum a spectrum showing dark lines at some narrow color regions (wavelengths). The lines are formed by atoms absorbing light, which lifts their electrons to higher orbits.

acceleration a change in an object's velocity (either its speed or its direction).

accretion addition of matter to a body. Examples are gas falling onto a star and asteroids colliding and sticking together.

accretion disk a nearly flat disk of gas or other material held in orbit around a body by its gravity.

active galaxy a galaxy whose central region emits abnormally large amounts of electromagnetic radiation from a small volume. Examples are radio galaxies, Seyfert galaxies, and quasars.

adaptive optics a technique for adjusting a telescope's mirror or other optical parts to compensate for atmospheric distortions, such as seeing, thereby giving a sharper image.

AGN an active galactic nucleus. The core of an active galaxy.

alpha particle a helium nucleus: two protons plus (usually) two neutrons.

altitude an object's angular distance above the horizon.

amino acid a carbon-based molecule used by living organisms to build protein molecules.

angstrom unit a unit of length used in describing wavelengths of radiation and the sizes of atoms and molecules. One angstrom $= 10^{-10}$ meters.

angular momentum a measure of an object's tendency to keep rotating and to maintain its orientation. Mathematically, it depends on the object's mass, M, radius, r, and rotational velocity, V, and is proportional to MVr.

angular size measure of how large an object *looks* to you. It is defined as the angle between lines drawn from the observer to opposite sides of an object. For example, the angular diameter of the Moon is about $\frac{1}{2}°$

annular eclipse an eclipse in which the body in front does not completely cover the other. In an annular eclipse of the Sun, a bright ring of the Sun's disk remains visible around the black disk of the Moon. We therefore see a ring (annulus) of light around the Moon.

anthropic principle the principle that the properties we observe the Universe to possess are limited to those that make our existence possible.

antimatter a type of matter that, if brought into contact with ordinary matter, annihilates it, leaving nothing but energy. The positron is the antimatter analog of the electron. The antiproton is the antimatter analog of the proton. Antimatter is observed in cosmic rays and can be created from energy in the laboratory.

aphelion the point in an orbit where a body is farthest from the Sun.

Apollo asteroids those asteroids whose orbits cross the Earth's.

association a loose grouping of young stars and interstellar matter, generally consisting of several star clusters.

asterism an easily identified grouping of stars, often a part of a larger constellation. For example, Orion's belt.

asteroid a small, generally rocky, solid body orbiting the Sun and ranging in diameter from a few meters to hundreds of kilometers.

asteroid belt a region between the orbits of Mars and Jupiter in which most of the Solar System's asteroids are located.

astronomical unit (AU) a distance unit based on the average distance of the Earth from the Sun.

atmospheric window a wavelength band in which our atmosphere absorbs little radiation. For example, on Earth the visible window ranges from about 300 to 700 nm, allowing the light we can see with our eyes to pass through the atmosphere.

atom a submicroscopic particle consisting of a nucleus and orbiting electrons. The smallest unit of a chemical element.

aurora the light emitted by atoms and molecules in the upper atmosphere. This light is a result of magnetic disturbances and appears to us as the northern or southern lights.

autumnal equinox the autumn equinox in the Northern Hemisphere. Fall begins on the autumnal equinox, which is on or near September 23.

averted vision the act of looking slightly to one side of a dim object so that you see it slightly away from the center of your field of view. This allows you to see a faint object better, although at a sacrifice of sharpness.

azimuth   a coordinate for locating objects on the sky. Azimuth is the angle measured from north along the horizon to the point below the object.

barred spiral galaxy   a galaxy in which the spiral arms wind out from the ends of a central bar rather than from the nucleus.

biased galaxy formation   a theory that galaxies form primarily in regions with a high density of cosmic matter.

Big Bang   the event that, according to many astronomical theories, created the Universe. It occurred about 15 billion years ago and generated the expanding motion that we observe today.

binary star   two stars in orbit around each other, held together by their mutual gravity.

bipolar flow   the narrow columns of high-speed gas ejected by a protostar in two opposite directions.

blackbody   an object that is an ideal radiator when hot and a perfect absorber when cool. It absorbs all radiation that falls upon it, reflecting no light; hence, it appears black. Stars are approximately blackbodies. The radiation emitted by blackbodies obeys Wien's law and the Stefan-Boltzmann law.

black dwarf   a collapsed star that has cooled to the point where it emits little or no visible radiation.

black hole   an object whose gravitational attraction is so strong that its escape velocity equals the speed of light, preventing light or any radiation or material body from leaving its "surface."

BL Lac object   a type of active galaxy named for the peculiar galaxy BL Lac. These objects generally are strong radio sources, and their visible light varies rapidly and erratically.

blueshift   a shift in the wavelength of electromagnetic radiation to a shorter wavelength. For visible light, this implies a shift toward the blue end of the spectrum. The shift can be caused by the motion of a source of radiation toward the observer or by the motion of an observer toward the source. For example, the spectrum lines of a star moving toward the Earth exhibit a blueshift. *See also* **Doppler shift.**

Bode's law   a numerical expression for the approximate distances of most of the planets from the Sun.

Bok globule   small, dark, interstellar cloud, often approximately spherical. Many globules are the early stages of protostars.

brown dwarf   a star that has a mass too low for it to begin nuclear fusion.

bulge   the dense, central region of a spiral galaxy.

carbonaceous chondrite   a type of meteorite containing many tiny spheres (chondrules) of rocky or metallic material stuck together by carbon-rich material.

CCD   charged-coupled device: an electronic device that records the intensity of light falling on it. CCDs have replaced film in most astronomical applications.

celestial equator   an imaginary line on the celestial sphere lying exactly above the Earth's equator. It divides the celestial sphere into northern and southern hemispheres.

celestial pole   an imaginary point on the sky directly above the Earth's North or South Pole.

celestial sphere   an imaginary sphere surrounding the Earth. Ancient astronomers pictured celestial objects as attached to it.

cepheid   a class of yellow-giant pulsating stars. Their pulsation periods range from about a day to about 70 days. Cepheids can be used to determine distances. *See also* **standard candle.**

Chandrasekhar limit   the maximum mass of a white dwarf. Approximately 1.4 solar masses. Named for the astronomer who first calculated that such a limit exists.

chondritic meteorite   a meteorite containing small spherical bodies called chondrules.

chondrule   a small spherical body embedded in a meteorite.

chromosphere   the lower part of the Sun's outer atmosphere that lies directly above the Sun's visible surface (photosphere).

cluster   a group of objects (stars, galaxies, and so forth) held together by their mutual gravitational attraction.

CNO cycle/process   a reaction involving carbon, nitrogen, and oxygen (C, N, and O) that fuses hydrogen into helium and releases energy. The process begins with a hydrogen nucleus fusing with a carbon nucleus. Subsequent steps involve nitrogen and oxygen. The carbon, nitrogen, and oxygen act as catalysts and are released at the end of the process to start the cycle again. The CNO cycle is the dominant process for generating energy in main-sequence stars that are hotter and more massive than the Sun.

coma   the gaseous atmosphere surrounding the head of a comet.

comet   a small body in orbit around the Sun, consisting of a tiny, icy core and a tail of gas and dust. The tail forms only when the comet is near the Sun.

compact stars   very dense stars whose radii are much smaller than the Sun's. These stars include white dwarfs, neutron stars, and black holes.

condensation   conversion of free gas atoms or molecules into a liquid or solid. A snowflake forms in our atmosphere when water vapor condenses into ice. (Technically, the word *deposition* is used to describe the conversion of gas to solid.)

conjunction   the appearance of two astronomical objects in approximately the same direction on the sky. For example, if Mars and Jupiter happen to appear near each other on the sky, they are said to be in conjunction. *Superior conjunction* refers to a planet that is approximately in line with the Sun but on the far side of the Sun from the Earth. *Inferior conjunction* refers to a planet that lies approximately between the Sun and the Earth.

conservation of angular momentum   a principle of physics stating that the angular momentum of a rotating body remains constant unless forces act to speed it up or slow it down. Mathematically, conservation of angular momentum states that MVR is a constant, where M is the mass of a body moving with a velocity V in a circle of radius R. One extremely important consequence of this principle is that if a rotating body shrinks, its rotational velocity must increase.

conservation of energy   a principle of physics stating that energy is never created or destroyed, although it may change its form. For example, energy of motion may change into energy of heat.

constellation   a grouping of stars on the night sky. Astronomers divide the sky into 88 constellations.

continuous spectrum   a spectrum with neither dark absorption nor bright emission lines. The intensity of the radiation in such a spectrum changes smoothly from one wavelength to the next.

convection   the rising and sinking motions in a liquid or gas that carry heat upward through the material. Convection is easily seen in a pan of heated soup on a stove.

convection zone   the region immediately below the Sun's visible surface in which its heat is carried by convection.

Coriolis effect   a deflection of a moving object caused by its motion across the surface of a rotating body. The Coriolis effect makes storms on Earth spin, generates large-scale wind systems, and creates cloud belts on many of the planets.

corona   the outer, hottest part of the Sun's atmosphere.

coronal hole   a low-density region in the Sun's corona. The solar wind may originate in these regions.

cosmic horizon   the maximum distance one can see out into the Universe at a given time. The horizon lies at a distance in light-years approximately equal to the age of the Universe in years.

cosmic microwave background (CMB)   the radiation that was created during the Big Bang and that permeates all space. At this time, the temperature of this radiation is 2.73 K.

cosmic rays   extremely energetic particles (protons, electrons, and so forth) traveling at nearly the speed of light. Some rays are emitted by the Sun, but most come from more distant sources, perhaps exploding supernovas.

cosmological constant   a term in the equations that Einstein developed to describe the structure of the Universe. The term has the effect of a repulsive "force" opposing gravity.

cosmological principle   the hypothesis that on average, the Universe looks the same to every observer, no matter where he or she is located in it.

cosmology   the study of the structure and evolution of the Universe.

Crab Nebula   a supernova remnant in the constellation Taurus. Astronomers in ancient China and the Far East saw the supernova explode in A.D. 1054. A pulsar lies in the middle of the nebula.

crater   a circular pit, generally with a raised rim and sometimes with a central peak. Crater diameters on the Moon range from centimeters to several hundred kilometers. Most craters on bodies such as the Moon are formed by the impact of solid bodies, such as asteroids.

critical density   the density necessary for a closed Universe. If the density of the Universe exceeds the critical density, the Universe will stop expanding and collapse. If the density is less than the critical density, the Universe will expand forever.

crust   the solid surface of a planet, moon, or other solid body.

curvature of space   the bending of space by a mass, as described according to Einstein's General Theory of Relativity. Black holes bend the space around them, curving it so that the region within the black hole is cut off from the rest of the Universe. The Universe too may be curved in such a way as to make its volume finite.

curved space   space that is not flat. *See also* **curvature of space.**

dark adaption   the process by which the eye changes to become more sensitive to dim light.

dark-line spectrum   a spectrum in which certain wavelengths are darker than adjacent wavelengths. The missing light is absorbed by atoms or molecules between the source and observer. Also called an *absorption-line spectrum.*

dark matter   matter that emits no detectable radiation but whose presence can be deduced by its gravitational attraction on other bodies.

dark nebula   a dense cloud of dust and gas in interstellar space that blocks the light from background stars.

daughter atoms   the atoms produced by the decay of a radioactive element. For example, uranium decays into lead. Thus, lead atoms are daughter atoms.

daylight saving time   the time kept during summer months by setting the clock ahead one hour. This gives more hours of daylight after the workday.

declination   one part of a coordinate system for locating objects in the sky north or south of the celestial equator. Declination is analogous to latitude on the Earth's surface.

degeneracy pressure   the pressure created in a dense gas by the interaction of its electrons. Degeneracy pressure does not depend on temperature.

degenerate gas   an extremely dense gas in which the electrons and nuclei are tightly packed. The pressure of a degenerate gas does not depend on its temperature.

density   the mass of a body or region divided by its volume.

density-wave theory of spiral structure   a theory to account for the spiral arms of galaxies. According to the theory, waves traveling through the disk of a galaxy sweep stars and interstellar gas into a spiral pattern.

differential gravitational force   the difference between the gravitational forces exerted on an object at two different points.

The effect of this force is to stretch the object. Such forces create tides and, if strong enough, may break up an astronomical object. *See also* **Roche limit.**

differentiation   the separation of different previously mixed materials inside a planet or other object. This is the same separation that occurs when a heavy material, for example iron, settles to the planet's core, leaving lighter material on the surface.

diffraction   a disturbance of light (or other electromagnetic waves) as it passes through an opening or around an obstacle. Diffraction limits the ability to distinguish fine details in images.

disk   the flat, round portion of a galaxy. The Sun lies in the disk of the Milky Way.

dispersion   the spreading of light or other electromagnetic radiation into a spectrum. A rainbow is an example of dispersion of light caused by raindrops.

DNA   deoxyribonucleic acid. The complex molecule that encodes genetic information in all organisms here on Earth.

Doppler shift   the change in the observed wavelength of radiation caused by the motion of the emitting body or the observer. The shift is an increase in the wavelength if the source and observer move apart and a decrease in the wavelength if the source and observer approach. *See also* **redshift** and **blueshift.**

dwarf   a small dim star.

dynamo   a physical process for generating magnetic fields in astronomical bodies. In many cases, the process involves the generation of electric currents from an interaction between rotation and convection.

Earth's magnetic field   the magnetism generated by the Earth. The magnetic field is what exerts the magnetic force on a compass needle.

eclipse   the blockage of light from one astronomical body caused by the passage of another between it and the observer. The shadow of one astronomical body falling on another. For example, the passage of the Moon between the Earth and Sun can block the Sun's light and cause a solar eclipse.

eclipse seasons   the times of year, separated by about 6 months, when eclipses are possible. At any given eclipse season, both a solar eclipse and lunar eclipse generally occur.

eclipsing binary   a binary star pair in which one star periodically passes in front of the other, totally or partially blocking the background star from view as seen from Earth.

ecliptic   the path followed by the Sun around the celestial sphere. The path gets its name because eclipses can only occur when the Moon crosses the ecliptic.

electric charge   the electrical property of objects that causes them to attract or repel one another. A charge may be either positive or negative.

electric force   the force generated by electric charges. It is attractive between unlike charges $(+-)$ but repulsive between like charges $(++$ or $--)$.

electromagnetic force   the force arising between electrically charged particles or between charges and magnetic fields. Forces between magnets are a special case of this force. This force holds electrons to the nucleus of atoms, makes moving charges spiral around magnetic field lines, and deflects a compass needle.

electromagnetic radiation   a general term to describe any kind of electromagnetic wave.

electromagnetic spectrum   the assemblage of all wavelengths of electromagnetic radiation. The spectrum includes the following wavelengths, from long to short: radio, infrared, visible light, ultraviolet, X rays, and gamma rays.

electromagnetic wave   a wave consisting of alternating electric and magnetic energy. Ordinary visible light is an electromagnetic wave, and the wavelength determines the light's color.

electron   a low-mass, negatively charged subatomic particle. Electrons orbit the atomic nucleus but may at times be torn free. *See also* **ionization.**

electroweak force   one of the fundamental forces of nature. At one time,

it was considered to be two separate forces: electromagnetism and the weak force. The weak force causes radioactive decay.

element   a fundamental substance, such as hydrogen, carbon, or oxygen, that cannot be broken down into a simpler chemical substance. Approximately 100 elements occur in nature.

ellipse   a geometric figure related to a circle but elongated in one direction.

elliptical galaxy   a galaxy in which the stars smoothly fill an ellipsoidal volume. Abbreviated E galaxy. The stars in such systems are generally old (Pop II).

emission   the production of light, or more generally, electromagnetic radiation by an atom or other object.

emission nebula   a hot gas cloud in interstellar space that emits light.

emission-line spectrum   a spectrum consisting of bright lines at certain wavelengths separated by dark regions in which there is no light.

energy   a quantity that measures the ability of a system to do work or cause motion.

energy level   any of the numerous levels that an electron can occupy in an atom, roughly corresponding to an electron orbit.

epicycle   a fictitious, small, and circular orbit superimposed on another circular orbit and proposed by early astronomers to explain the retrograde motion of the planets.

equator   the imaginary line that divides the Earth (or other body) symmetrically into its northern and southern hemispheres. The equator is perpendicular to a body's rotation axis.

equinox   the time of year when the number of hours of daylight and night are approximately equal. The spring and fall (vernal and autumnal) equinoxes mark the beginning of the spring and fall seasons.

escape velocity   the speed an object needs to move away from another body in order not to be pulled back by its gravitational attraction. Mathematically, the escape velocity, V, is defined as

$$\sqrt{\frac{2GM}{R}}$$

where M is the body's mass, R is its radius, and G is the gravitational constant.

eukaryotes cells with nuclei. Most cells in current terrestrial organisms have nuclei and are thus eukaryotes.

Evening star any bright planet, often Venus, seen low in the western sky after sunset.

event horizon the location of the "surface" of a black hole. An outside observer cannot see in past the event horizon.

excited the condition in which the electrons of an atom are not in their lowest energy level (orbit).

exclusion principle the condition that no more than two electrons may occupy the same energy state in an atom. This limitation leads to degeneracy pressure.

extra-solar planet a planet not orbiting our Sun.

falsecolor picture/photograph a depiction of an astronomical object in which the colors are not the object's real colors. Instead, they are colors arbitrarily chosen to represent other properties of the body, for example, the intensity of radiation, which we cannot see.

false vacuum a state of the early Universe.

fission the splitting of a single body, such as an atom, into two or more pieces.

flare an outburst of energy on the Sun. *See also* **solar flare.**

flat universe a universe that extends forever with no curvature. Its total energy is zero.

fluorescence the conversion of ultraviolet light (or other short-wavelength radiation) into visible light.

focus (1) one of two points within an ellipse used to generate the elliptical shape. The Sun lies at the focus of each planet's elliptical orbit. (2) a point in an optical system in which light rays are brought together. The location where an image forms in such systems.

frequency the number of times per second that a wave vibrates.

fundamental forces the three basic forces of nature: gravitation, the electroweak force, and the strong force. According to some modern theories (*see also* **GUTs**), these three forces are different forms of a single, more fundamental, unified force.

Gaia hypothesis the hypothesis that life does not merely respond to its environment but actually alters its planet's atmosphere and temperature to make the planet more hospitable. For example, by photosynthesis, plants have created an oxygen-rich atmosphere on Earth, which shields the plants from dangerous ultraviolet radiation. Gaia is pronounced *Guy-uh* in this context.

galactic cannibalism the capture and merging of one galaxy into another.

galaxy a massive system of stars held together by their mutual gravity. Typical galaxies have a mass between about 10^7 and 10^{13} solar masses. Our galaxy is the Milky Way.

galaxy cluster a group of galaxies held together by their mutual gravitational attraction. The Milky Way belongs to the Local Group galaxy cluster.

Galilean satellites the four moons of Jupiter discovered by Galileo: Io, Europa, Ganymede, and Callisto.

geocentric centered on the Earth. Many of the earliest attempts to describe the Solar System were geocentric in that they supposed that the planets moved around the Earth rather than around the Sun.

giant a star of large radius and large luminosity.

glitches abrupt changes in the pulsation period of a pulsar, perhaps the result of adjustments of its crust.

globular cluster a dense grouping of old stars, containing generally about 10^5 to 10^6 members. They are often found in the halos of galaxies.

globule *see* **Bok globule.**

grand unified theories (GUTs) theories that propose that in the early Universe, all the fundamental forces behaved as a single force.

granulation texture seen in the Sun's photosphere. Granulation is created by clumps of hot gas that rise to the Sun's surface.

grating a piece of material that creates a spectrum by reflecting light from or passing it through many very fine and closely spaced parallel lines.

gravitational lens an object that bends space (and thereby the light passing through the space) by its gravitational attraction and focuses the light to create an image of a more distant object. *See also* **curvature of space.**

gravitational redshift the shift in wavelength of electromagnetic radiation (light) created by a body's gravitational field as the radiation moves away from the body. Only extremely dense objects, such as white dwarfs, produce a significant redshift of their radiation.

gravitational waves a wavelike bending of space generated by the acceleration of massive bodies.

gravity the force of attraction that is between two bodies and is generated by their masses.

greatest elongation the position of an inner planet (Mercury or Venus) when it lies farthest from the Sun on the sky. Mercury and Venus are particularly easy to see when they are at greatest elongation. Objects may be at greatest eastern or western elongation according to whether they lie east or west of the Sun.

greenhouse effect the trapping of heat by a planet's atmosphere, making the planet warmer than would otherwise be expected. Generally, the greenhouse effect operates if visible sunlight passes freely through a planet's atmosphere, but the infrared radiation produced by the warm surface cannot escape readily into space.

Gregorian calendar the calendar devised at the request of Pope Gregory XIII and essentially the civil calendar used throughout the world today. It omits the leap year for century years not divisible evenly by 400.

GUTs   *see* **grand unified theories.**

halo   the approximately spherical region surrounding spiral galaxies that contains mainly old stars, such as the globular clusters. The halo may also contain large amounts of dark matter.

Hawking radiation   radiation that black holes are hypothesized to emit as a result of quantum effects. This radiation leads to the extremely slow evaporation of black holes.

heliocentric   centered on the Sun. Used to describe models of the Solar System in which the planets orbit the Sun.

helium flash   the beginning of helium fusion in a low-mass star. The fusion begins explosively and causes a major readjustment of the star's structure.

Herbig-Haro objects   clumps of gas seen near some young stars.

highlands   the old, heavily cratered regions on the Moon.

horizon   the line separating the sky from the ground. *See also* **cosmic horizon.**

H-R diagram   a graph on which stars are located according to their temperature and luminosity. Most stars on such a plot lie along a diagonal line, called the main sequence, which runs from cool, dim stars in the lower right, to hot, luminous stars in the upper left.

Hubble constant   the multiplying constant H in the Hubble law, $V = HD$. The reciprocal of the Hubble constant (in appropriate units) is approximately the age of the Universe.

Hubble law   a relation between a galaxy's distance, D, and its recession velocity, V, which states that more distant galaxies recede faster than nearby ones. Mathematically, $V = HD$, where H is the Hubble constant.

hydrogen burning   nuclear fusion of hydrogen into helium. It is not "burning" like ordinary fire but is instead the transformation of one kind of atom into another accompanied by the release of energy.

hydrostatic equilibrium   the condition in which pressure and gravitational forces in a star or planet are in balance. Without such balance, bodies will either collapse or expand.

hypothesis   an explanation proposed to account for some set of observations or facts.

HII region   a region of ionized hydrogen. HII regions generally show a luminous pink/red glow and often surround luminous, hot, young stars.

ideal gas law   a law relating the pressure, density, and temperature of a gas. This law states that the pressure is proportional to the density times the temperature. Also called the *perfect gas law*.

inclination   the tilt angle of an astronomical object or its orbit.

inertia   the tendency of an object at rest to remain at rest and of a body in motion to continue in motion in a straight line at a constant speed. *See also* **mass.**

inferior conjunction   *see* **conjunction.**

inferior planet   a planet whose orbit lies between the Earth's orbit and the Sun. Mercury and Venus are inferior planets.

inflation   the rapid expansion of the early Universe by an enormous factor.

infrared   a wavelength of electromagnetic radiation longer than visible light but shorter than radio waves. We cannot see these wavelengths with our eyes, but we can feel many of them as heat. The infrared wavelength region runs from about 1000 nm to 1 mm.

inner core   the innermost part of a planet, also called the *solid core*. The Earth's inner core is a mixture of solid iron and nickel.

inner planet   a planet orbiting in the inner part of the Solar System. Sometimes taken to mean Mercury, Venus, Earth, and Mars.

instability strip   a region in the H-R diagram in which stars pulsate.

interferometer   a device consisting of two or more telescopes connected together to work as a single instrument. Used to obtain a high resolving power, the ability to see small-scale features. Interferometers may operate at radio, infrared, or visible wavelengths.

international date line   an imaginary line from the Earth's north to south pole, running approximately down the middle of the Pacific Ocean. It marks the location on Earth at which the date changes.

interstellar cloud   a cloud of gas and dust in between the stars. Such clouds may be many light years in diameter.

interstellar grain   microscopic solid dust particles in interstellar space. These grains absorb starlight, making distant stars appear dimmer than they truly are.

interstellar matter   matter in the form of gas or dust in the space between stars.

inverse-square law   (1) any law in which some property varies inversely as the square of the distance, d. Mathematically, as $1/d^2$. (2) the law stating that the apparent brightness of a body decreases inversely as the square of its distance.

ionization   the removal of one or more electrons from an atom, leaving the atom with a positive electric charge. Under some circumstances, an extra electron may be attached to an atom, in which case the atom is described as negatively ionized.

ionized   a condition in which the number of an atom's electrons does not equal the number of its protons. Typically, this means the atom is missing one or more electrons.

irregular galaxy   a galaxy lacking a symmetric structure.

jets   narrow streams of gas ejected from any of several types of astronomical objects. Jets are seen near protostars and in many active galaxies.

jet stream   a narrow stream of high-speed wind that blows in the atmosphere of a planet. Such winds occur on Earth and many other planets.

joule   a unit of energy. One joule per second equals one watt.

Jovian planet   one of the giant, gaseous planets: Jupiter, Saturn, Uranus, and Neptune. The name *Jovian* was chosen because Jupiter's structure is representative of the other three.

Julian calendar   a 12-month calendar devised under the direction of Julius Caesar. It includes a leap year every four years.

Kepler's three laws   laws that describe the motion of planets around the Sun. The first law states that planets move in elliptical orbits with the Sun off center at a focus of the ellipse. The second law states that a line joining the planet and the Sun sweeps out equal areas in equal times. The third law relates a planet's orbital period, P, to the semimajor axis of its elliptical orbit, a. Mathematically, the law states that $P^2 = a^3$, if P is measured in years and a in astronomical units.

Kirkwood gaps   regions in the asteroid belt with a lower-than-average number of asteroids. Some of the gaps result from the gravitational force of Jupiter removing asteroids from orbits within the gaps.

Kuiper belt   a region from which some comets come. The region appears to extend from the orbit of Neptune, past Pluto, out to approximately 55 AU.

law of gravity   a description of the gravitational force exerted by one body on another. The gravitational force is proportional to the product of their masses and the inverse square of their separation. If the masses are M and m and their separation is d, the force between them, F, is $F = GMm/d^2$, where G is a physical constant.

light   electromagnetic energy.

light-year   a unit of distance equal to the distance light travels in one year. A light-year is roughly 10^{13} km, or about 6 trillion miles.

liquid core   the molten interior of a planet, also called the *outer core*.

lobes   regions lying outside the body of a radio galaxy where much of its radio emission comes from.

Local Group   the small group of about 30 galaxies to which the Milky Way belongs.

Local Supercluster   the cluster of galaxy clusters in which the Milky Way is located. The Local Group is one of its member clusters.

luminosity   the amount of energy radiated per second by a body. For example, the wattage of a light bulb defines its luminosity. Stellar luminosity is usually measured in units of the Sun's luminosity (approximately 4×10^{26} watts).

lunar eclipse   the passage of the Earth between the Sun and the Moon so that the Earth's shadow falls on the Moon.

Magellanic clouds   two small companion galaxies of the Milky Way.

magnetic field   a representation of the means by which magnetic forces are transmitted from one body to another.

magnetic lines of force   fictitious lines used to visualize the orientation and strength of a magnetic field.

magnetosphere   the extreme upper regions of the Earth's atmosphere in which the motion of the gas is controlled by the Earth's magnetic field.

magnitude   a unit for measuring stellar brightness. The smaller the magnitude, the brighter the star.

main sequence   the region in the H-R diagram in which most stars, for instance the Sun, are located. The main sequence runs diagonally across the H-R diagram from cool, dim stars to hot, luminous ones. Stars on the main sequence fuse hydrogen into helium in their cores. *See also* **H-R diagram.**

main-sequence lifetime   the time a star remains a main sequence star, fusing hydrogen into helium in its core.

mantle   the solid, outer part of a planet. This part is immediately below the crust.

mare   a vast, smooth, dark, and congealed lava flow filling a basin on the Moon and on some planets. Maria often have roughly circular shapes.

maria   plural of *mare*.

maser   an intense radio source created when excited gas amplifies some background radiation. "Maser" stands for *m*icrowave *a*mplification by *s*timulated *e*mission of *r*adiation.

mass   a measure of the amount of material an object contains. A quantity measuring a body's inertia.

mass function   the number of stars of a given mass range in some group.

mass-luminosity relation   a relation between the mass and luminosity of stars. Higher-mass stars have higher luminosity.

Maunder minimum   the time period from about A.D. 1600 to 1740 during which the Sun was relatively inactive. Few sunspots were observed during this period.

mean solar day   the standard 24 hour day. The mean solar day is based on the average day length over a year. (The time interval from sunrise to sunrise varies slightly throughout the year).

megaparsec   a distance unit equal to 1 million parsecs and abbreviated Mpc.

metal   astronomically, any chemical element more massive than helium. Thus, carbon, oxygen, iron, and so forth are metals.

meteor   the bright trail of light created by small solid particles entering the Earth's atmosphere and burning up. A "shooting star."

meteor shower   an event in which many meteors occur in a short space of time, all from the same general direction in the sky. The most famous shower is the Perseids in mid-August.

meteorite   the solid remains of a meteor that falls to the Earth.

meteoroid   the technical name for the small, solid bodies moving within the Solar

System. When a meteoroid enters our atmosphere and heats up, the trail of luminous gas it leaves is called a meteor. When the body lands on the ground, it is called a meteorite. ("A meteoroid is in the void. A meteor above you soars. A meteorite is in your sight.")

method of standard candles   *See* standard candle.

Mid-Atlantic ridge   an underwater mountain range on Earth created by plate-tectonic motion and running approximately north-south down the center of the Atlantic Ocean.

Milky Way galaxy   the galaxy to which the Sun belongs. Seen from Earth, the galaxy is a pale, milky band in the night sky.

Miller-Urey experiment   an experimental attempt to stimulate the conditions under which life might have developed on Earth. Miller and Urey discovered that amino acids and other complex organic compounds could form from the gases that are thought to have been present in the Earth's early atmosphere, if the gases are subjected to an electric spark or ultraviolet radiation.

millisecond pulsar   a pulsar whose rotation period is about a millisecond.

minute of arc   a measure of angle equal to one-sixtieth of a degree.

model   a theoretical representation of some object or system.

molecule   two or more atoms bonded into a single particle, such as water, H_2O (two hydrogen atoms bonded to one oxygen) or carbon dioxide, CO_2 (one carbon atom bonded to two oxygen atoms).

Moon illusion   the illusion that the Moon appears larger when near the horizon than when see high in the sky.

Morning star   any bright planet visible in the eastern sky before dawn.

nanometer   a unit of length equal to 1 billionth of a meter (10^{-9} meters) and abbreviated nm. Wavelengths of visible light are several hundred nanometers. The diameter of a hydrogen atom is roughly 0.1 nm.

neap tide   the abnormally small tide occurring when the Sun's and Moon's gravitational effects on the ocean partially offset each other.

nebula   cloud in interstellar space.

negative curvature   a form of curved space sometimes described as being open in that it has no boundary. Negative curvature is analogous to a saddleshape.

neutrinos   tiny neutral particles with little or no mass and immense penetrating power. These particles are produced in great numbers by the Sun as it fuses hydrogen into helium and also by some supernova explosions.

neutron   a subatomic particle of nearly the same mass as the proton but with no electric charge. Neutrons and protons comprise the nucleus of the atom.

neutron star   a very dense, compact star composed primarily of neutrons.

Newton's first law of motion   a body continues in a state of rest or uniform motion in a straight line unless made to change that state by forces acting on it. *See also* inertia.

Newton's second law of motion $F = ma$. In words, the amount of acceleration, a, that a force, F, produces depends on the mass, m, of the object being accelerated.

Newton's third law of motion   when two bodies interact, they exert equal and opposite forces on each other.

nonthermal radiation   radiation emitted by charged particles moving at high speed in a magnetic field. The radio emission from pulsars and radio galaxies is nonthermal emission. More generally, nonthermal means "not due to high temperature."

north celestial pole   the point on the celestial sphere sky directly above the Earth's North Pole. Objects on the sky appear to circle around this point.

North Star   any star that happens to lie very close to the north celestial pole. Polaris has been the North Star for about 1000 years, and it will continue as such for about another 1000 years, at which time a star in Cepheus will be nearer the north celestial pole.

nova   a process in which a surface layer of hydrogen builds up on a white dwarf and then fuses explosively into helium. Nova explosions do not destroy the star and may be recurrent.

nuclear force   the force that holds protons and neutrons together in the atomic nucleus. Also called the *strong force*.

nuclear fusion   the binding of two light nuclei to form a heavier nucleus with some nuclear mass converted to energy. For example, the fusion of hydrogen into helium. This process supplies the energy of most stars and is commonly called "burning" by astronomers.

nucleosynthesis   the formation of elements, generally by the fusion of lighter elements into heavier ones. For example, the formation of carbon by the fusion of three helium nuclei.

nucleus   the core of an atom around which the electrons orbit. The nucleus has a positive electric charge and comprises most of an atom's mass.

nucleus of galaxy   the central region of a galaxy.

obscuration   the blocking of light of background stars by interstellar matter.

occultation   the covering up of one astronomical body by another. For example, the Moon passes directly between Earth and the planets from time to time, covering them up and causing their occultation.

Olbers' paradox   an argument that the sky should be bright at night because of the light from many distant stars and galaxies.

Oort cloud   a vast region in which comet nuclei orbit. This cloud lies far beyond the orbit of Pluto.

opacity   the blockage of light or other electromagnetic radiation by matter.

open cluster   a loose cluster of stars, generally containing a few hundred members.

opposition   the configuration of a planet when it is opposite the Sun in the sky. If a planet is in opposition, it rises when the Sun sets and sets when the Sun rises.

orbit the path in space followed by a celestial body; also a description of an electron's position in an atom.

outer core the molten interior of a planet; also called the *liquid core.*

outer planet a planet whose orbit lies in the outer part of the Solar System. Jupiter, Saturn, Uranus, Neptune, and Pluto are outer planets.

ozone a form of oxygen consisting of three oxygen atoms bonded together. Its chemical symbol is O_3. Because it absorbs ultraviolet radiation, ozone in our atmosphere shields us from the Sun's harmful ultraviolet radiation.

panspermia a theory that life originated elsewhere than on Earth and came here across interstellar space either accidently or deliberately.

parallax the shift in an object's position caused by the observer's motion. A method for finding distance based on that shift.

parsec a unit of distance equal to about 3.26 light-years (3.09×10^{13} km) defined as the distance at which an observer sees the maximum angle between the Sun and the Earth to be one arc second.

perfect gas law a law relating the pressure, density, and temperature of a gas. It states that the pressure is proportional to the density times the temperature. This is also called the *ideal gas law.*

perihelion the point in an orbit closest to the Sun.

period the time required for a repetitive process to repeat. For example, orbital period is the time it takes a planet or star to complete an orbit. Pulsation period is the time it takes a star to expand and then contract back to its original radius.

period-density relation a relation that states that the period of a variable star is inversely proportional to the square root of its average density. That is, high-density stars pulsate more rapidly than low-density stars.

period-luminosity law a law stating that the longer the period of a pulsating variable star, the more luminous it is.

phases the changing illumination of the Moon or other body that causes its apparent shape to change. The following is the cycle of lunar phases: new, crescent, first quarter, gibbous, full, gibbous, third quarter, crescent, new.

photo dissociation the breaking apart of a molecule by intense radiation.

photon a particle of visible light or other electromagnetic radiation.

photosphere the visible surface of the Sun. When we look at the Sun in the sky, we are seeing its photosphere.

planet a body in orbit around a star.

planetary nebula a shell of gas ejected by a low-mass star late in its evolutionary lifetime. Planetary nebulas typically appear as a glowing gas ring around a central star.

planetesimal one of the numerous small, solid bodies that, when gathered together, form a planet.

plate tectonics the hypothesis that the crust of the Earth (or some other planet) is divided into large regions (plates) that move very slowly over the planet's surface. Interaction between plates at their boundaries creates mountains and activity such as volcanoes and earthquakes.

polarity the property of a magnet that causes it to have a north and south pole.

poor cluster a galaxy cluster with a small number of members. The galaxy cluster to which the Milky Way belongs, the Local Group, is a poor cluster.

population (Pop) I the younger stars, some of which are blue, that populate a galaxy's disk, especially its spiral arms.

population (Pop) II the older, redder stars that populate a galaxy's halo and bulge.

population (Pop) III a hypothetical stellar population consisting of the first stars that formed in a galaxy, composed of only hydrogen and helium.

positive curvature bending of space leading to a finite volume. A space that is "closed." A universe with positive curvature is analogous to a spherical shape.

positron a subatomic particle of antimatter with the same mass as the electron but a positive electric charge. It is the electron's antiparticle.

powers-of-ten notation a shorthand way to write numbers using ten to a power. For example, $1,000,000 = 10^6$. Also called *scientific notation.*

precession the slow change in direction of the pole (rotation axis) of a spinning body.

pressure the force exerted by a substance such as a gas on an area divided by that area. That is, pressure $\times$ area = force.

prokaryotes cells without nuclei. Presumably the first life forms on Earth were prokaryotes.

prominence a cloud of hot gas in the Sun's outer atmosphere. This cloud is often shaped like an arch.

protein any of many complex organic molecules composed of a chain of amino acids. Proteins serve many functions in cells, including structure and metabolism.

proton a positively charged subatomic particle. One of the constituents of the nucleus of the atom.

proton-proton chain the nuclear fusion process that converts hydrogen into helium in stars like the Sun and thereby generates their energy. This is the dominant energy-generation mechanism in cool, low-mass stars.

protostar a star still in its formation stage.

pulsar a spinning neutron star that emits beams of radiation that happen to sweep across the Earth each time the star spins. We observe the radiation as regularly spaced pulses.

pulsate to expand and contract regularly. For example, pulsating variable stars swell and shrink in a predictable, regular fashion.

quantized the property of a system that allows it to have only discrete values.

quasar a peculiar galaxy characterized by a large redshift, high luminosity, and an extremely small, active core. Quasars are among the most luminous and most distant objects known to astronomers.

radial velocity the velocity of a body along the line of sight. That is, the part of its motion directly toward or away from the observer.

radiant the point in the sky from which meteors in showers appear to come. *See also* **meteor showers.**

radiation pressure the force exerted by radiation on matter.

radiative zone the region inside a star where its energy is carried outward by radiation (that is, photons).

radio galaxy a galaxy, generally an elliptical system, that emits abnormally large amounts of radio energy. *See also* **lobes.**

radioactive decay the breakdown of an atomic nucleus by the emission of subatomic particles.

radioactive element an element that undergoes radioactive decay and breaks down into a lighter element.

radius of the Universe a distance that measures the approximate "size" of the Universe. It is roughly the distance light can travel in a time equal to the Universe's age.

rays long, narrow, light-colored markings on the Moon or other bodies that radiate from young craters. Rays are debris "splashed" out of the crater by the impact that formed it.

recession velocity the velocity of an external galaxy (or other object) away from the Sun.

recombination the reattachment of one (or more) electrons to an atom following its removal.

reddening the alteration in a star's color as seen from Earth as the star's light passes through an intervening interstellar dust cloud. The dust preferentially scatters the blue light from the beam, leaving the remaining light redder.

red giant a cool, luminous star whose radius is much larger than the Sun's.

redshift a shift in the wavelength of electromagnetic radiation to a longer wavelength. For visible light, this implies a shift toward the red end of the spectrum. The shift can be caused by a source of radiation moving away from the observer or by the observer moving away from the source. For example, if a star is moving away from Earth, its spectrum lines exhibit a redshift. *See also* **Doppler shift.**

reflection nebula an interstellar cloud in which the dust particles reflect starlight, making the cloud visible.

reflector a telescope that uses a mirror to collect and focus light.

refraction the bending of light when it passes through one substance and enters another.

refractor a telescope that uses a lens to collect and focus light.

regolith the surface rubble of broken rock on the Moon or other solid body.

resolving power the ability of a telescope or instrument to discern fine details. Larger-diameter telescopes have greater (that is, better) resolving power.

resonance a condition in which the repetitive motion of one body interacts with the repetitive motion of another so as to reinforce the motion. Sliding back and forth in a bathtub to make a big splash is an example.

retrograde motion the drift of a planet westward against the background stars. Normally, planets shift eastward because of their orbital motion. The planet does not actually reverse its motion. The change in its direction is caused by the change in the position from which we view the planet as the Earth overtakes and passes it.

rich cluster a galaxy cluster containing hundreds to thousands of member galaxies.

rifting the breaking apart of a continental plate.

right ascension a coordinate for locating objects on the sky, analogous to longitude on the Earth's surface. Measured in hours and minutes of time.

rilles narrow canyons on the Moon or other body.

ring galaxy a galaxy in which the central region has an abnormally small number of stars, causing the galaxy to look like a ring. Caused by the collision of two galaxies.

Roche limit the distance from an astronomical body at which its gravitational force breaks up another astronomical body.

rotation axis an imaginary line through the center of a body about which the body spins.

rotation curve a plot of the rotation velocity of the stars or gas in a galaxy at different distances from its center.

RR Lyrae stars a type of white, giant, pulsating variable star with a period of about one day or less. They are named for their prototype star, RR Lyrae.

satellite a body orbiting a planet.

scattering the random redirection of a light wave or photon as it interacts with atoms or dust particles.

Schwarzschild radius the radius of a black hole. The distance from the center of a black hole to its event horizon.

scientific method the process of observing a phenomenon, proposing a hypothesis on the basis of the observations, and then testing the hypothesis.

scientific notation *see* **powers-of-ten notation.**

scintillation the twinkling of stars.

seeing a measure of the steadiness of the atmosphere during astronomical observations. Under conditions of bad seeing, fine details are difficult to see. Bad seeing results from atmospheric irregularities moving between the telescope and the object being observed.

seismic waves waves generated in the Earth's interior by earthquakes. Similar waves occur in other bodies. Two of the more important varieties are S and P waves. The former can travel only through solid material; the latter can travel through either solid or liquid material.

selection effect an unintentional selection process that omits some set of the objects being studied and leads to invalid conclusions about the objects.

self-propagating star formation a model that explains spiral arms as arising from stars triggering the birth of other stars around them. The resulting pattern is then drawn out into a spiral by the galaxy's rotation.

semimajor axis half the long dimension of an ellipse.

SETI Search for *Extra*terrestrial *Intelligence.* Some such searches involve automatic "listening" to millions of radio frequencies for signals that might be from other civilizations.

Seyfert galaxy variety of active galaxy with a small, abnormally bright nucleus containing hot gas. Named for the astronomer Carl Seyfert, who first drew attention to these objects.

shell source a region in a star where the nuclear energy generation occurs around the core rather than in it.

shepherding satellite one or more satellites that by their gravitational attractions prevent particles in a planet's rings from spreading out and dispersing. Saturn's F-ring is held together by shepherding satellites.

short-period comet a comet whose orbital period is shorter than 200 years. For example, Halley's comet has a period of 76 years.

sidereal day the length of time from the rising of a star until it next rises. The length of the Earth's sidereal day is 23 hours 56 minutes.

sidereal period the time it takes a body to turn once on its rotation axis or to revolve once around a central body, as measured with respect to the stars.

sidereal time a system of time measurement based on the motion of stars across the sky rather than the Sun.

silicates material composed of silicon and oxygen, and generally containing other substances as well. Most ordinary rocks are silicates. For example, quartz is silicon dioxide.

solar cycle the cyclic change in solar activity, such as sunspots and solar flares.

solar day the time interval from one sunrise to the next sunrise or from one noon to the next noon. That time interval is not always exactly 24 hours but varies throughout the year. For that reason, we use the mean solar day (which, by definition, is 24 hours) to keep time.

solar eclipse the passage of the Moon between the Earth and the Sun so that our view of the Sun is partially or totally blocked. *See also* **total eclipse.**

solar flare a sudden increase in brightness of a small region on the Sun. This flare is caused by a magnetic disturbance.

solar nebula the rotating disk of gas and dust from which the Sun and planets formed.

solar nebula hypothesis the hypothesis that the Solar System formed from a rotating cloud of gas and dust, the solar nebula.

Solar System the Sun, planets, their moons, and other bodies that orbit the Sun.

solar wind the outflow of low-density, hot gas from the Sun's upper atmosphere. It is partially this wind that creates the tail of a comet by blowing dust and gas away from the comet's immediate surroundings.

solid core the inner iron-nickel core of the Earth or other planet. Despite its high temperature, the core is solid because it is under great pressure. Also called the *inner core.*

solstice (winter and summer) the beginning of winter and summer. Astronomically the solstice occurs when the Sun is at its greatest distance north (June) or south (December) of the celestial equator.

south celestial pole the imaginary point on the celestial sphere directly over the Earth's South Pole.

spectral class an indicator of a star's temperature. A star's spectral class is based on the appearance of its spectrum lines. The fundamental classes are, from hot to cool, O, B, A, F, G, K, and M.

spectrograph a device for making a spectrum.

spectroscopic binary a type of binary star in which the spectrum lines exhibit a changing Doppler shift as a result of the orbital motion of one star around the other.

spectroscopy the study and analysis of spectra.

spectrum electromagnetic radiation (for example, visible light) spread into its component wave-lengths or colors. The rainbow is a spectrum produced naturally by water droplets in our atmosphere.

spicule a hot, thin column of gas in the Sun's chromosphere.

spiral arm a long, narrow region containing young stars and interstellar matter that winds outward in the disk of spiral galaxies.

spiral galaxy a galaxy with a disk in which its bright stars form a spiral pattern.

spring tide the abnormally large tides that occur at new and full moon.

standard candle a type of star or other astronomical body in which the luminosity has a known value, allowing its distance to be determined by measuring its apparent brightness and applying the inverse-square law: for example, Cepheid variable stars, supernovas, and so forth.

standard time a uniform time kept within a given region so that all clocks there agree.

star a massive, gaseous body held together by gravity and generally emitting light. Normal stars generate energy by nuclear reactions in their interiors.

star cluster   a group of stars numbering from hundreds to millions held together by their mutual gravity.

steady-state theory   a model of the Universe in which the overall properties of the Universe do not change with time.

Stefan-Boltzmann law   the amount of energy radiated from one square meter in one second by a blackbody of temperature T is proportional to T^4.

strong force   the force that holds protons and neutrons together in the atomic nucleus. Also called *nuclear force*.

subatomic particles   particles making up an atom, such as electrons, neutrons, and protons, or other particles of similar small size.

subduction   the sinking of one crustal plate where it encounters another.

sunspot   a dark, cool region on the Sun's visible surface created by intense magnetic fields.

supercluster   a cluster of galaxy clusters. Our Milky Way belongs to the Local Group, a small galaxy cluster that is but one of many galaxy groups making up the Local Supercluster.

superfluidity   a condition in which a fluid has no friction (technically, the absence of viscosity).

supergiant   a very large-diameter and luminous star, typically at least 10,000 times the Sun's luminosity.

superior conjunction   *see* **conjunction.**

superior planet   a planet orbiting farther from the Sun than the Earth. Mars, Jupiter, Saturn, Uranus, Neptune, and Pluto are superior planets.

supernova   an explosion marking the end of some star's evolution. Astronomers identify two main kinds of supernovas: Type I and II. Type I occurs in a binary system in which one star is a white dwarf. The explosion is triggered when mass from a companion star falls onto the white dwarf, raising its mass above the Chandrasekhar limit and causing the star to collapse. Collapse heats the white dwarf so that its

carbon and oxygen fuse explosively, destroying the star and leaving no remnant. Type II probably occurs when a massive star's iron core collapses. A Type II supernova leaves either a neutron star or a black hole, depending on the mass of the collapsing core.

supernova remnant   the debris ejected from a star when it explodes as a supernova. Typically, this material is hot gas, expanding away from the explosion at thousands of kilometers or more per second.

surface gravity   the acceleration caused by gravity at the surface of a planet or other body.

synchronous rotation   the condition that a body's rotation period is the same as its orbital period. The Moon rotates synchronously.

synchrotron radiation   a form of nonthermal radiation emitted by charged particles spiraling at nearly the speed of light in a magnetic field. Pulsars and radio galaxies emit synchrotron radiation. The radiation gets its name because it was first seen in synchrotrons, a type of atomic accelerator.

synodic period   the time between successive configurations of a planet or moon. For example, the time between oppositions of a planet or between full moons.

tail   the plume of gas and dust from a comet. The plume is produced by the solar wind and radiation pressure acting on the comet. The tail points away from the Sun and gets longer as the comet approaches perihelion.

terrestrial planet   a rocky planet similar to the Earth in size and structure. The terrestrial planets are Mercury, Venus, Earth, and Mars.

tidal braking   the slowing of one body's rotation as a result of gravitational forces exerted on it by another body.

tidal bulge   a bulge on one body created by the gravitational attraction on it by another. Two tidal bulges form, one on the side near the attracting body and one on the opposite side.

tides   the rise and fall of the Earth's oceans created by the gravitational attraction of the Moon. Tides also occur in the solid crust of a body and its atmosphere.

time zone   one of 24 divisions of the globe every 15 degrees of longitude. In each zone, a single standard time is kept. Most zones have irregular boundaries.

total eclipse   an eclipse in which the eclipsing body totally covers the other body. Only at a total solar eclipse can we see the Sun's corona.

transit   the passage of a planet directly between the observer and the Sun. At a transit, we see the planet as a dark spot against the Sun's bright disk. From Earth, only Mercury and Venus can transit the Sun.

triangulation   a method for measuring distances. This method is based on constructing a triangle, one side of which is the distance to be determined. That side is then calculated by measuring another side (the base line) and the two angles at either end of the base line.

triple alpha process   the fusion of three helium nuclei (alpha particles) into a carbon nucleus. This process is sometimes called helium burning, and it occurs in many old stars.

T Tauri star   a type of extremely young star that varies erratically in its light output.

tuning-fork diagram   a diagram devised by Hubble to classify the various forms of spiral, elliptical, and irregular galaxies. The diagram is named for its shape.

turnoff point   the location on the main sequence where a star's evolution causes it to move away from the main sequence toward the red giant region. The location of the turnoff point can be used to deduce the age of a star cluster.

type I supernova   *see* **supernova**

21-cm line   a spectrum line at radio wavelengths produced by un-ionized (neutral) hydrogen.

ultraviolet   a portion of the electromagnetic spectrum with wavelengths shorter than that of visible light but longer than that of X rays. By convention, the ultraviolet region extends from about 10 to 300 nm.

Universal time   the time kept at Greenwich, England. Universal time is the same as Greenwich mean time. Most local times (in the United States, these are Eastern, Central, Mountain, Pacific, and so forth) differ from it by an even number of hours.

Universe the largest astronomical structure we know of. The Universe contains all matter and radiation and encompasses all space.

Van Allen radiation belts doughnut-shaped regions surrounding the Earth containing charged particles trapped by the Earth's magnetic field.

variable star a star whose luminosity changes in time.

vernal equinox the spring equinox in the Northern Hemisphere. Spring begins on the vernal equinox, which is on or near March 21.

visible spectrum the part of the electromagnetic spectrum that we can see with our eyes. It consists of the familiar colors red, orange, yellow, green, blue, and violet.

visual binary star a pair of stars held together by their mutual gravity and in orbit about each other, and which can be seen with a telescope as separate objects.

visual double star two stars that appear to lie very close together on the sky but in reality are at greatly different distances.

wavelength the distance between wavecrests. It determines the color of visible light and is generally denoted by the Greek letter λ.

wave-particle duality the theory that electromagnetic radiation may be treated as either a particle (photon) or an electromagnetic wave.

weak force the force responsible for radioactive decay of atoms. Now known to be linked to electric and magnetic forces and therefore called the electroweak force.

white dwarf a dense star whose radius is approximately the same as the Earth's but whose mass is comparable with the Sun's. White dwarfs burn no nuclear fuel and shine by residual heat. They are the end stage of stellar evolution for stars like the Sun.

white light visible light exhibiting no color of its own but composed of a mix of all colors. Sunlight and many artificial light sources are "white."

Wien's law a relation between a body's temperature and the wavelength at which it emits radiation most intensely. Hotter bodies radiate more intensely at shorter wavelengths. Mathematically, the law states that $\lambda_m = 3 \times 10^6/T$, where λ_m is the wavelength of maximum emission in nanometers and T is the body's temperature on the Kelvin scale.

X-ray binaries a binary star system in which one of the stars, or the gas associated with a star, emits X rays intensely. Such systems generally contain a collapsed object such as a neutron star or a black hole. *See also* **X-ray burster.**

X-ray burster a stellar system producing repetitive outbursts of X-ray radiation. X-ray bursters are thought to consist of a neutron star and a normal star in a close binary system. Mass from the normal star spills onto the neutron star, where it slowly accumulates and heats. Eventually, the temperature becomes large enough to initiate nuclear fusion. The released energy heats the material further, causing more fusion and leading to an explosion that we observe as the X-ray burst.

year the time that it takes the Earth to complete its orbit around the Sun; that is, the period of the Earth's orbit.

Zeeman effect the splitting of a single spectrum line into two or three lines by a magnetic field. A method for detecting magnetic fields in objects from their radiation.

zenith the point on the celestial sphere that lies directly overhead at your location.

zodiac a band running around the celestial sphere in which the planets move.

zone of avoidance a band running around the sky in which few galaxies are visible. It coincides with the Milky Way and is caused by dust that is within our galaxy. This dust blocks the light from distant galaxies.

Index

Note: Page number references refer to the customized JROTC Astronomy student textbook.